This book, *Lead Differently*, is an [...] Next-Gen leaders. Out with the business model and in with [...] the biblical model. It should seem obvious that church leaders would lead like Jesus, but for decades we've been told to hone our corporate leadership skills. Who better than Larry Titus to write this insightful and simply revolutionary leadership book? Add it to your library as I have added it to mine. Let's remove our traditional filter and make a difference as we embrace intelligent thought that is theologically sound and simply applied.

Dr. Tony Evans
President, The Urban Alternative
Senior Pastor, Oak Cliff Bible Fellowship

Lead Differently by Dr. Larry Titus is no ordinary book on the leadership style of Jesus, but rather a profound, in-depth tutorial on how to instantly recognize the way to gain influence as a leader. This book teaches you what is the next step for your development—using the exact same leadership road Jesus Himself traveled down. If you're satisfied with your current level of leadership, then this is not a book for you. But if your heart cries out to become a life-changing, Godly leader, then this is the book that can lead you there!

Marcus D. Lamb
Founder and President
Daystar Television Network

Larry Titus is a leader, but he is more than that, he is a spiritual father, mentor, and teacher. His life and his leadership are marked by scars of sacrificial obedience to Jesus Christ. I know of no one more qualified to speak to us on the aspects of leading like Jesus. I was challenged and motivated in my own leadership by reading this book and you will be too.

Tom Lane
Apostolic Senior Pastor
Gateway Church
Southlake, Texas

Prepare to be confronted, challenged and changed by an encounter with a lifetime of kingdom experience, a revelation of biblical exposition, and a unique prophetic exhortation—all of which will enhance the call of God on your life as a gifted leader.

Don't read this book if you are committed to static leadership. If you are comfortably resting on the laurels of past organizational accomplishments, this book is not for you.

If you have a sneaking suspicion that God wants to do exceeding, abundantly more through you than you have seen as a Kingdom leader, then this book is for you, for your organization, and for the people you lead.

Kenneth C. Ulmer, PhD, DMin
Trustee, The King's University
Presiding Bishop
Macedonia International Bible Fellowship

I have read many books on leadership and have attended numerous leadership conferences. Having been thoroughly blessed by your concepts and understanding, I am going to require the entire Christ for the Nations staff to read Pastor Larry Titus' book on leadership. This book touched me, as it will you. Trust me—after you read it, you will see what I mean.

Dr. Dennis Lindsay
President & CFO, Christ for the Nations

My friend Larry Titus is one of the greatest Christian leaders I know, so it is no surprise that his new book *Lead Differently* is filled with clear, compelling, and poignant insights to help us follow Jesus' pattern for leadership, something he's done effectively for close to sixty years. I couldn't put the book down! I encourage you to read it, apply it, and commit to leading differently so that those under your care can come into their full destiny, and together as the Ekklesia, we can see the Great Commission fulfilled in our generation.

Dr. Ed Silvoso
Author, *Ekklesia: Rediscovering God's Instrument for Global Transformation*
Founder, Transform Our World

There are many books, conferences, and seminars on leadership. But in such a time as this, leaders will need to Lead Differently. Through this book, Larry Titus issues a clarion call and a detailed framework for anyone to learn to lead like Jesus and have a profound impact on this world.

Dr. Dwayne Cantrell
Senior Pastor, Living Victory Church
Associate Vice President, California State University, Bakersfield

One of the church's foremost developers of leadership around the world, Larry leverages his years of successful kingdom development with a powerful but simple framework for effective leadership. Featuring Jesus as the world's most effective leader, the principles outlined in these pages are simple, effective, practical and easily applied. The opportunity to lead like Jesus is before us. I know this book will enhance the vision of effective leadership for chaotic times.

Jim Hennesy
Lead Pastor, Trinity Church, Cedar Hill, Texas

God has called you to be a great leader, and it starts by leading like the world's greatest leader, Jesus Christ. Grounded in scripture and filled with amazing insight and wisdom, this book will equip you to become a successful leader in every area of your life. I am grateful my good friend Larry Titus wrote this book, and I know you will be too!

Robert Morris
Senior Pastor, Gateway Church
Bestselling Author of *The Blessed Life, Beyond Blessed,* and *Take the Day Off*

LEAD
DIFFERENTLY

Discover how
leading
like
Jesus
can work for you

LARRY TITUS

Lead Differently

Published by HigherLife Development Services Inc.
PO Box 623307
Oviedo, Florida 32762
www.ahigherlife.com

ISBN: 978-1-954533-26-4 (Paperback)
978-1-954533-27-1 (ebook)
Library of Congress Control Number: 2021909106

10 9 8 7 6 5 4 3 2 1

Printed in the United States of America

Table of Contents

To my wife: Devi Titus
To my children: Trina Titus Lozano and Aaron Titus
To my grandchildren: Brooke Sailer, Brandon Lozano,
Brittany White, Bryson Lozano, Melody Titus, and
Michaela Titus
To my great-grandchildren:
Sophia Sailer, Isabella Sailer, Brielle Sailer, Liam Sailer
Levi Lozano, Landon Lozano, Eliana Lozano,
Anderson White, Faith White, Haven White, Maisy White
and several more great-grandchildren
who are yet to be born.
Nothing is more important to me than my family.

Acknowledgments

To My Wife, Devi

How many men are fortunate enough to have married an editor, a publisher, a housewife, a companion, a model, a mother, a grandmother, a great-grandmother, a speaker, a cook, an interior designer, an encourager, a corrector, an inspiration, and, like the Holy Spirit, a comforter and helper?

For 57 years of marriage and ministry, Devi has been all of that and much more to me. Her insights are woven throughout this book, both spoken and unspoken. Her wisdom permeates every page. Her spiritual discernment and deep convictions have long been the plumb-line in my life and ministry. Without her, nothing I have accomplished could have been possible.

I'm more than blessed.

To the Indispensable Three

To those who assisted me in writing, editing, correcting, and offered valuable insights into this manuscript, I am so grateful:

Jennifer Strickland, Larry V. Lee, and Jeff Hamilton. Muchas gracias, Muito obrigado, Vielen Dank, Merci beaucoup, Bol'shoye spasibo, and Toda raba. Roughly translated, these words mean, "You're awesome and I love you."

To Jesus Christ

The love of my life is Jesus Christ. Absolutely nothing of meaning, value, or eternal substance would have been possible without my Savior, and certainly not this book. He has healed me times without number, physically, emotionally, and spiritually. He threw my sins into the Sea of Forgetfulness, never to be remembered again. Thank God for God.

He taught me sonship and the love of the Father.

He shared His anointing and authority with me.

His ongoing covering of blood forgives and cleanses me daily. His edible body, the Word of God, is my daily sustenance, and His earthly Body, the Church, is a constant source of blessing, relationships, and refinement. I can hardly wait for the day when I will physically kneel before Him and cry, "Jesus, you are Lord!"

Introduction

This is a book for normal people—people who aspire to greatness but have counted themselves out. People who would like to be successful leaders but don't think they have the gifts, talents, passion, abilities, personality, or skills required to become one.

I have good news for you. Jesus, the world's greatest leader, was just like you. When He chose to divest Himself of His royal privileges, He also made the choice to become like you in every way. Hebrews 2:17 says that Jesus "had to be made like his brothers in every respect." That means that Jesus was normal.

How can an average man, Jesus, become the world's greatest leader? It wasn't because He was God. Philippians 2:5-9 makes clear that Jesus emptied Himself of everything that demanded equality with the Father and became a servant. When Jesus became incarnate, He retained nothing of His heavenly privileges.

How can Jesus Christ, one of the lowliest, most unlikely of leaders, become the greatest leader in human history? It's because He *led differently* from most leaders, ancient and modern. He had a different rule book. He followed a different set of patterns and principles. His truths were not of this world's system. He was born to die.

I've followed the Man from Galilee for 74 years. I was born again when I was four years old. I began in leadership positions when I was eighteen years old. I've followed the leadership principles of Jesus for sixty years.

I've started works from zero and saw them succeed. I've taken over ministries that were splintered, broken, and divided and brought them into health and productivity.

I've invested in leaders from dozens of nations and witnessed their transformation and fruitfulness.

I've believed in leaders that others had rejected, recognized their anointing, and released them into their calling.

I've loved leaders when their past failures convinced them their ministry was over, only to see it revive and flourish.

Conversely, I've at times led with a heavy hand, insensitive to the needs of the people. I've selfishly put my interests ahead of theirs and experienced embarrassment and dismal failure, proof that I should have *led differently* and more *effectively*.

Lead Differently dissects the life of Jesus revealed in the Gospels and breaks it down in to the leadership principles that made Him the world's greatest leader.

I am convinced that if you follow the same principles taught and revealed by Jesus you will experience the same success that Jesus had.

Wasn't it Jesus who promised that if you would believe in Him, the works that He did you would do also, and even greater works you would do (John 14:12-14)?

I believe it's because Jesus *led differently*. You will notice that every chapter of this book contains biblical wisdom that literally defies many modern books on leadership. If you're interested in seeing yourself as an effective, reproductive leader, and to see everyone you lead completely, diametrically changed, challenged, and groomed for greatness, then this book is for you.

If you don't read another chapter in this book, read the first chapter. Though I'm convinced the first chapter will "hook" you and you'll find yourself compelled to read the rest of the book, I assure you, you will never be the same. I've written every chapter with one goal and that was to see your leadership style transformed.

If you follow the leadership style of Jesus, you will succeed. You have no other choice. No other options. If you do what Jesus did, you will have the success that Jesus had. But you must *lead differently*.

If you're a dictatorial, coercive, controlling leader, you'll either have to change your style of leadership or be content to have short-lived success and immature followers. It's like having a big head with a small body. The head continues to grow but the body remains the same, incapable of coming into maturity. I'm convinced this book will give you an option you will want to consider.

If you're a mild-mannered leader, content to let others do what you should be doing, often abdicating your responsibility, you'll find yourself feeling emboldened, encouraged, and ready to get out of the boat, take charge, change your world, and *lead differently.*

If you've experienced only mediocre success, this book will change your mindset from "I'll probably never, ever be a great leader, God has consigned me to smallness," to "I can do that too. Who says I have to be a small leader with a small vision? Why should I be content with smallness? Jesus *led differently* and so can I."

If you're insecure in your leadership role, you will find yourself emboldened to tackle any obstacle and take down any giant. God is a master at taking weakness and turning it into strength. You will find your insecurity being exchanged for confidence as you *lead differently.*

If you're a mega-pastor, with a mega-personality, leading a mega-church, on mega-campuses, viewed on mega-television stations, attracting mega-crowds and adoring multitudes, you might find yourself wanting to escape from the trap of constant demands by people and a crushing program into the relaxation of *leading differently.*

Whatever leadership style or personality you have, the principles of Jesus Christ will fit your personality and release your calling.

God called you to greatness as a leader. Don't stop short. But you must *lead differently.*

Please know that I'm behind you. I'll be praying for you that God will use you powerfully to see His kingdom come to your family, church, community, city, and nation. Remember, you and Jesus make a majority if you will *lead differently*.

I believe in you,

Larry Titus

CHAPTER 1

Lead
with humility

*Self is the opaque veil that
hides the face of God from us.*

Richard J. Foster

*"Father, if you are willing, remove this cup from me.
Nevertheless, not my will, but yours, be done."*

Luke 22:42

Jesus Christ of Nazareth never promoted Himself. Let me repeat that: Jesus Christ of Nazareth never promoted Himself! Let me shout it: *Jesus Christ of Nazareth never promoted Himself!* Did you get it? Am I speaking a foreign language? Is this soaking in? Are you comprehending this truth? Let's say it in a different way.

The world's greatest leader never sought to promote or advance His own agenda.

He didn't seek publicity, but avoided it.

He had no interest in popularity. He was accustomed to people hating Him. He told those He healed not to tell anyone. He rebuked those who tried to get Him to show off His miraculous power. He managed to offend just about everyone, including His own family and disciples.

When someone called Him "great," He deferred, saying "only my Father is great."

The religious sects hated Him, and sinners loved Him.

He rejected all creature comforts, including a bed, a pillow, a home, and money.

He never sought to do His own will, follow His own vision, or establish His own kingdom.

Jesus had only one goal in life, and that was to die.

Have you ever seen a leader like Jesus? More importantly, do you lead like Jesus?

If I were to ask you the one thing that made Jesus of Nazareth the world's greatest leader, what would you say it would be? What is the key to His success?

Out of the seven billion people living in the world today, over two billion follow a leader who lived two thousand years ago. Why?

What is the one thing that Jesus did that no other leader in the history of the world has ever done, or at least to the degree that Jesus did?

What is your answer?

Can you guess?

If you were to do one thing that would embody and encapsulate the leadership principles of Jesus, what would it be?

I know the answer, and soon you will know the answer, too. Thoroughly read these verses.

When Jesus was 12 years old
"Did you not know that I must be in my Father's house, about my Father's business?" (Luke 2:49, with footnote).

In His early ministry
"My food is to do the will of him who sent me and to accomplish his work" (John 4:34).

When Jesus was accosted by the Pharisees
"Truly, truly, I say to you, the Son can do nothing of his own accord, but only what he sees the Father doing. For whatever the Father does, that the Son does likewise" (John 5:19).

"I can do nothing on my own. As I hear, I judge, and my judgment is just, because I seek not my own will but the will of him who sent me" (John 5:30).

To the Jews
"Jesus said to them, 'When you have lifted up the Son of Man, then you will know that I am he, and that I do nothing on my own authority, but speak just as the Father taught me'" (John 8:28).

After Jesus fed the 5,000
"For I have come down from heaven, not to do my own will but the will of him who sent me" (John 6:38).

The night before Jesus was crucified
"And going a little farther he fell on his face and prayed, saying, 'My Father, if it be possible, let this cup pass from me; nevertheless, not as I will, but as you will'" (Matthew 26:39).

> There has never
> been a leader in
> human history
> whose sole purpose
> in life was to do the
> will of another.

No One Like Him

There has never been a leader in human history whose sole purpose in life was to do the will of another. His only motivation in life was to do the will of His Father in heaven. Even with the knowledge that His decision would lead to death on a cross, He never wavered from His ultimate goal.

Do you see how contradictory this attitude is to modern practice? What leader would spend his or her entire life seeking to do the will of someone else? Do you see how revolutionary this concept is? Is this the key most of us have been missing? We've been taught to promote ourselves, push our vision, establish our goals, and passionately pursue our purpose in life.

Everyone who begins their ministry with a "me first" approach will find themselves at odds with the model of Jesus. If selfish pursuit, doing your will first and foremost, is your priority, you've already broken the most important leadership principle in the life of Jesus.

If your concept of leadership is to subscribe to your own vision, the foundation of your motivation can be self-motivated, and "not my will," becomes "my will, first!" The end result of all things built on self-centeredness is self-destruction. Sooner or later, "self" will "self-destruct." All vision and ministry built on "not my will, but yours be done" is built on the will of the Father and the Son. This leads to fruitfulness that is both eternal and reproducible. God has a perfect plan for your life. If you say "yes" to His will, His plan will unfold before you and you will experience true fulfillment.

Though it may sound simplistic, there are only two leadership styles: Spirit-led leadership and self-led leadership. They are not only opposites, they are violently opposed to each other.

Spirit-led leadership is selfless and seeks only to do the will of the Father and others you work for and serve, such as your employer, spouse, congregation, etc.

Self-led leadership is self-centered, self-promoting, and only seeks to do the will of your own vision.

Spirit-led leadership seeks to find the source of its vision from the will of the Father.

Self-led leadership finds motivation in passionate pursuit of what is most gratifying to the flesh and soul.

Spirit-led leadership finds ultimate joy in promoting God and others.

Self-led leadership finds ultimate joy in the applause and accolades of man.

Spirit-led leadership is deeply satisfying.

Self-led leadership is hollow, and satisfaction is temporary.

Selfish Ambition

I know of nothing more destructive to leadership than selfish ambition. James 3:16 says, "For where jealousy and selfish ambition exist, there will be disorder and every vile practice."

In addition to your pursuit of the will of God first and foremost, your leadership success will also be determined by how much and how well you promote the ministry and vision of others as well, keying in on God's plan for their lives.

This type of character development begins in early childhood, when a child is taught to do the will of its parents over its own will.

It follows them into their teens when they get their first jobs. How much do you desire to do the will of your boss rather than your own will?

For all of us who consider serving the Master full-time as our calling, it is critical that we seek to do His will 100% of the time, at all times subjugating our will to that of the Father. Our chief enemy will always be the temptation of self-promotion. It doesn't come easily or naturally for us to seek to do the will of another, yet herein lies the key to our future success.

The world's most selfless individual became the world's greatest leader.

> If anyone's will is to do God's will, he will know whether the teaching is from God or whether I am speaking on my own authority. *The one who speaks on his own authority seeks his own glory*, but the one who seeks the glory of him who sent him is true, and in him there is no falsehood. (John 7:17-18, emphasis added)

Did you get that? Jesus said that a person cannot even know whether His teaching is credible unless he seeks to do God's will over his own.

Unfortunately, many leaders spend their entire lives seeking to fulfill "their" vision, only to be confronted with disappointment and disillusionment.

The Power of Selfless Leadership

Though Jesus was only thirty years of age when He began to teach, and He taught for only a few years, His life and teaching have impacted the world. In addition to His followers, millions of people who don't consider themselves followers of Jesus have been impacted in one way or another by those who do. Hospitals, churches, schools, universities, humanitarian causes, literature, music, architecture, science, and even Western civilization itself continue to carry the influence of the man from Galilee. It's hard to imagine any nation in the world where the influence of Jesus and His teaching has not reached in some form. Even our reckoning of years is based on His birth.

What makes Jesus the world's greatest leader?

How can one man change the course of history?

Jesus didn't write any books, He didn't marshal an army, He didn't have a financial strategy, He didn't overthrow a government, He didn't lead a rebellion, He never founded a religion, and He didn't erect any buildings or memorials to Himself.

In His three and a half years of ministry, Jesus preached to the multitudes only on rare occasions, spoke to crowds mostly in His final eighteen months, and spent most of His time training twelve fairly unqualified men, eleven from the uneducated north of Israel.

He had no possessions other than the clothing He wore and no pillow to rest His head in slumber.

He was rejected by His family, His hometown sought to kill Him, He was considered to be demon-possessed by the religious leaders, betrayed by His treasurer, and was forsaken in His final hours by His remaining eleven disciples. The only title He had was written in derision and nailed on a board to the top of the cross on which He was crucified. He was exchanged for a murderer and His only companions on adjoining crosses were thieves, one of whom railed against Him in His final hours. His tormentors bartered for His only possession, His robe, while taunting the healer with the ultimate insult, "Physician, heal yourself."

While He was on the cross, His Father turned His back on Him from 12-3 p.m. as He took upon Himself the sins of the world. What was left?

He was buried in a borrowed tomb.

The Sin of Self-Promotion

Self is that integral part of our nature that loves to be exalted and praised. Self loves to hear our names spoken out loud in a public setting or see them in print, especially large print. Self never tires of praise and recognition!

An amazing quality of the world's greatest leader is that He never promoted Himself. In fact, He did everything in His power to promote everyone other than Himself, primarily the

> ## Self is that integral part of our nature that loves to be exalted and praised.

Father. While His disciples attempted to exalt Him on the stage of public opinion, Jesus prepared Himself to be lifted up on a cross (John 12:32).

Jesus made it clear in John 5:31 that if He promoted Himself, it would invalidate His ministry. His documented life establishes this precedent. "If I alone bear witness about myself, my testimony is not true." Likewise, this could be true of the rest of us as well. While we are busy self-promoting, we are simultaneously making our ministry invalid as well as demoting God. Heaven refuses to praise us when we praise ourselves.

The most selfless thing we can ever do is the will of someone else. When that "someone else" is God the Father, we take the first step toward becoming great leaders. With this step, we become people who lead others into the fullness of God; we lead those around us from darkness to light. A leader aligned with God's will goes before and breaks ice for His followers, setting them free from cold immobility. Our goal should be to make Jesus and His will our top priority.

When we die to self and elevate the will of God, we become equipped to authentically lead others.

Imagine a conversation like this:

"What do you want to do when you grow up?"

"Oh, I'd like to do the will of God rather than my own will. I'd rather fulfill His desires and not my own. That's all I've ever wanted to do. In my whole life I've only desired to do God's will."

Are you kidding me? Who would say that? Moreover, who would say that and then *do* it? In all of history, we know of one person who said that and actually did it—Jesus, the world's greatest leader.

If we could go back and interview Jesus for the *Jerusalem Post*, it would probably sound like this:

Interviewer: "Jesus, what are your main goals in life?"
Jesus: "I plan on doing the will of my Father."
Interviewer: "What is your five-year plan?"
Jesus: "It's like my first-, second-, third-, and fourth-year plan. I plan on doing the will of my Father."
Interviewer: "But don't you have any plans of your own?"
Jesus: "That is a plan of my own. I decided in eternity that I would lay aside all of my prerogatives and do only the will of my Father. I plan on doing the will of my Father, now, tomorrow, and for the rest of my life."

In my 60 years of ministry, I've asked dozens of young aspiring preachers what they would like to accomplish in their future. I've heard many say they want to be apostles, prophets, pastors, teachers, evangelists, or missionaries. I've heard few people say they just want to serve the ministry of another.

Neither have I heard an employee say their chief desire in life is to see their employer succeed.

If you can't follow
the vision of another,
God will never give
you your own.

Why? There is something intrinsic in our self-nature that desires self-promotion. Who would propose that their stated purpose in life was to do the will of another? But that's exactly what Jesus did. *Is it possible that herein lies the secret to all leadership?*

Are we willing to seek the welfare and success of the one we serve before seeking our own?

No wonder so many ministries are aborted before they begin. They begin with the assumption that if I build my ministry first, then everything else will fall into place. I'm here to suggest that if you're unwilling to seek first the success of another, you will never find true success yourself.

If you can't follow the vision of another, God will never give you your own.

Nothing sets apart the leadership principles of Jesus from other leaders more than that statement. Jesus never came to do His own will, follow His own vision, or determine His own destiny. From the time Jesus was twelve years of age, His only will was to do the will of His Father.

If you start off your ministry career with selfish ambition, you will continue to bear the fruit of selfish ambition. If you seek first the welfare of another, as Jesus did, the self-life will have to give way to the selfless life, producing fruit that endures.

Not My Will, but Yours

A leader must first make himself small and others great before he will ever become great. To truly live, he must be willing to sacrifice his own life for those he leads.

Jesus embodies the world's true pattern for leadership. As a leader, he risked His life for the Father's will while at the same time loving His men. As a child, He was keenly aware that His only goal in life was to fulfill the will of the Father. He even thought it strange that His parents did not recognize this. Luke 2:49 says, "Did you not know that I must be in my Father's house?" From the age of twelve to His final words in the garden, "Father, not my will but yours be done," Jesus never strayed from this singleness of purpose. It was never "Me first," but always, "My Father first." According to the pattern Jesus left us, to attain true greatness in leadership, you must first be willing to honor and promote the leadership of another.

When the disciples returned from grabbing their Big Macs at the Samaritan version of McDonald's, Jesus said, "I have food to eat that you know nothing about." Notice now His response to the disciples' inquiry: "My food," said Jesus, "is to do the will of him who sent me and to finish his work" (John 4:32, 34 NIV). More important than the daily sustenance of bread was to do the will of the Father.

All the way to Gethsemane, Jesus held steadfastly to His conviction that He would defer to God the Father and do His will.

This is important! A deep change in your church, your work life, and your family is near at hand and depends upon the nature of your leadership. Godly leaders sweep away selfish ambitions. Godly leaders lead differently.

I've heard people say, pray, or sing, "God, I give you my will." Though it may sound spiritual, it's really impossible. You can't give away your will. If God took away your will, you'd be a robot. You were born with a "will" and that "will" never stops "willing" until you breathe your last breath. Your will is what defines you. It's your ability to make decisions. It's your determination. It's your personality. It's who you are. God doesn't want your will; He wants your willingness to align your will to His will.

Your will is what determines who you choose to promote, either God's plan for your life or your own.

I say to you, without equivocation, that if you choose to do God's will over your own, you will establish your leadership and discover your ultimate destiny.

God wants to align your will with His. No matter how great your plans are, they aren't His. You can't even determine your next breath, or the events of tomorrow. By saying, "Jesus, I don't want to do my will; I want only to do yours," you start to line up with God.

Let's make it even simpler: if you do God's will, you will finally find fulfillment. Self-seeking and self-promotion will not satisfy you. In losing yourself, you will find yourself, period. It's God's method.

How well known would Mother Teresa be today if she had chosen something other than feeding starving children in India?

Would the father of our nation, George Washington, have succeeded had he chosen the comfortable fireplace of Mt. Vernon over the chill of Valley Forge? Praying over the starving and shoeless soldiers in the camp is not my idea of an idyllic Christmas holiday. George Washington was the first elected president of our democracy. But do you know what really made him special? He preferred the needs of his men over his own comfort; he held together a ragtag army by his selfless example, and his men followed him all the way to Yorktown and one of the greatest victories in American history, thereby ending the Revolutionary War.

More importantly, would two billion people today be following Jesus of Nazareth had He chosen His own will over that of the Father? I can answer definitively and unequivocally: absolutely not! The leader who follows "self" disqualifies himself from leadership; ultimately, people will see him as either weak and insipid or despotic and dictatorial.

Jesus didn't reach for equality with His Father. In fact, the Apostle Paul says that Jesus did not consider equality with the Father something to be grasped. The Greek word for "grasped" (*harpagmos*) is telling—it actually has a violent connotation, that of obtaining equality through robbery. Jesus did not try stealing equality from the Father. "Though he was in the form of God, [he] did not count equality with God a thing to be grasped, but emptied himself, by taking the form of a servant, being born in the likeness of men" (Philippians 2:6-7).

Are we anywhere near to Jesus' degree of purity and selflessness? No. Self wants public recognition. Self wants to be seen. Self wants to be in control. That's the nature of self. Leaders motivated by self follow the self-examples or role models they've seen. Positions of honor, accolades from peers, public recognition, fame, and wealth are the common goals of selfish leaders.

The Deception of Self

If you desire to be a great leader, study and apply Philippians 2:5-9. Jesus emptied Himself of something. What was it? Contrary to the opinion of some authors, Jesus did not empty Himself of Deity. God can never become "not-God." Jesus was fully God and fully man. "For in him the whole fullness of deity dwells bodily" (Colossians 2:9; see also Colossians 1:19; Hebrews 1:3).

Jesus emptied Himself of everything that promoted *self* over the Father! He never demanded equality with the Father but humbled Himself to the point where His will was completely subordinated to that of the Father.

Nothing is more contrary to the will of God than being motivated by "self." It opposes God at every turn. Selfish or self-centered people filter their decisions through the sieve of self-benefit and self-aggrandizement. What is the result? Selfish leadership results in deception, disappointment, and confusion. These leaders judge themselves by how others see them. Therefore, such leaders are always disoriented and given to the swirling misdirection of political approval.

Most scholars believe that the person the prophet Isaiah is referring to in Isaiah 14:12-14 is none other than Satan himself: "How are you fallen from heaven, O Day Star, son of

Dawn! . . . You said in your heart, 'I will ascend to heaven, above the stars of God. I will set my throne on high; I will sit on the mount of assembly in the far reaches of the north; I will ascend above the heights of the clouds; I will make myself like the Most High.'"

Notice the self-deception displayed in self-exaltation. Of course, Satan would never have been content to be *like* God or even *equal* with God. He wouldn't have been satisfied until He was seated above God and God was subservient to him. He wanted to *be* God.

Selfishness is never content to be *equal*. It always demands total dominance. Like Satan, we might say we want *equality*, but as soon as *self* rears its head, *supremacy* becomes the true goal.

When Jesus came as God to this earth, He came in love. Love was Jesus' paradigm, and through love He laid down every form of selfishness and only did the will of His Father.

As long as self sits as king on the throne of your life, you will forever be relegated to the bonfire of failure. Self-centeredness always fails, no matter what direction you pursue. It is as simple as a mathematical function. *If you input selfishness, you will output misery and very painful failure and loss.*

Selfishness Begins at Birth

A child comes out of the womb with a selfish nature. I'm convinced that the first word ever uttered from the mouths of most babies, immediately following the adorable "Momma" and "Dadda," is the resounding and demanding "*mine!*" Then, two tiny, chubby hands tenaciously grasp for the toy of another

Selfishness never leads to happiness. It leads to depravity.

adorable baby who is also screaming, *"mine!"* Cute, aren't they? Who are we kidding? Self asserts its desire for kingship from the crib.

I couldn't believe the teeth marks my beautiful, sweet, innocent, darling, little toddler-daughter, Trina, left on the wrist of the little boy in the church nursery when he tried taking away "her" toy. *"Mine!"* she screamed, with teeth bared. "Mine, you little devil. I'll bite you until I get it!" My wife and I were horrified at the damage done by our adorable angel. How could she? Yet, she acted only out of her early human nature. Self-based impulses took control and her ownership of the toy caused her to believe in "mine." Sin is baked into our early personality. We need redemption from our original selves.

Most sadly, as we head into our lives and journey from grade school through to the marriage altar, our compass still points in the direction of "mine." I've seen family members fighting over the casket of their dead father or mother. Even the shock and finality of death can't stop self from raising its ugly head. Before the casket was even lowered into the grave, the relatives were screaming, *"mine!"*

Lives led by the mantra "I did it my way" are filled with heartbreak, divorce, broken relationships, chaos, alcoholism, drug addiction, loneliness, and suicide. Selfishness never leads to happiness. It leads to depravity. It pays dividends of spiritual, emotional, and physical ruin. Navigation through life, guided by self, leads you in the opposite direction from God. You don't want to be there.

James 3:16 says, "For where jealousy and selfish ambition exist, there will be disorder and every vile practice." Therefore, self-based living and selfish ambitions open us to demonic influence. We play right into Satan's hands if we exalt ourselves. I cannot emphasize this enough: run from selfish ambition like you are running from the fires of hell! You don't want to be there!

The world's greatest leader never thought or fought to do His own will. It's hard to comprehend, isn't it? Jesus had to overcome all of fallen creation, including man, beast, and satanic minions, to win the war of the "will."

Always keep the life of Jesus in mind, for He defines how we should lead our own lives.

Selfless Leadership Produces Serving Leaders

Jesus issued a scathing rebuke to the Pharisees in Luke 11:43 because "you love the best seat in the synagogues and greetings in the marketplaces." The antidote for self-promotion is found three chapters later in Luke 14:8-11, when Jesus taught: "When you are invited by someone to a wedding feast, do not sit down in a place of honor, lest someone more distinguished than you be invited by him, and he who invited you both will come and say to you, 'Give your place to this person,' and then you will begin with shame to take the lowest place. But when you are invited, go and sit in the lowest place, so that when your host comes he may say to you, 'Friend, move up higher.' Then you will be honored in the presence of all who sit at table with you. For everyone who exalts himself will be humbled, and he who humbles himself will be exalted."

Selfless leaders are not produced by self-promoting leaders. Look again at what life has shown us. False leadership, based on themes other than the will of God, taints all downstream development of other leaders. There is a truly frightening incongruence and carnality in leaders developed by misguided leadership upstream. Have you felt your own reactions to such leaders? There is an unsettled discomfort deep within us when we hear these leaders.

I pray that God helps us be like Jesus, the world's most selfless leader. No wonder His disciples would follow Him to death—and they did. All of the disciples except John the Beloved died as martyrs for Jesus. What greater affirmation can be given for the authenticity of Jesus' life and leadership?

The Self-Life Displayed

Here are a few notorious behaviors that are fruits of self-based living and leadership:

- Boasting, in all its forms, is a display of self.
- Greed—doing things for financial gain—is an outgrowth of the self-based life.
- Possessiveness (*"Mine!"*) is a dead give-away.
- Rapacity, taking something by force, is linked to the Latin word, rape, being 100% self-gratifying.
- Arrogance screams, "Look at me!" while the selfless leader says, "Look at Him!"

- An obsessive fixation on our own appearance breeds self-focus, which dims our ability to see others clearly.

All grocery items have a "shelf" life, an expiration date, printed on them, anywhere from a few days or weeks to a few months. The "self life," however, has no expiration dates. Selfishness and egocentricity are life-long temptations and must continually be submitted to the cross. Just as we maintain the health of our bodies, we must maintain our hearts by continually putting others ahead of ourselves.

Selfishness is the most destructive force in the universe, even viler than greed. It is worth repeating: "For where you have envy and selfish ambition there you find disorder and every evil practice" (James 3:16 NIV).

It is no wonder that Jesus completely emptied Himself of everything that demanded "Me first" and put the Father's will first in every circumstance.

The Secret of a Great Leader

Compassionately seeking the welfare of another before one's own, is the secret of a great leader. Jesus laid aside His divine prerogatives, humbled Himself, and became obedient to the Father. In seeking the will of another, Jesus modeled the path to becoming a great leader.

Years ago, a young man came to me requesting to be hired as a youth pastor in our local congregation. My answer to him was probably something he wasn't expecting: "If you will put my vision first ahead of your own, I'll hire you." I knew that if he were to start out selfishly pursuing his own goals, he would

Promoting others will open the door for your own promotion.

fail. When he agreed to my demands, I hired him. Then, *my* leadership goal became to see him released in *his* vision—and he flourished.

I've since moved from that city, and he went on to be an incredible youth pastor, at my recommendation, in another congregation. Do I need to say that his youth ministry exploded in growth? A man who seeks the will of another over his own will see the fruit of his labor expressed in an abundant harvest.

I am absolutely convinced that God will not promote any person who spends their time promoting themselves.

Promoting others will open the door for your own promotion. Self-promotion takes God out of the picture. If you promote yourself, anything you accomplish won't come from a fresh spring of bubbling water; it will taste stale and bitter. *You cannot simultaneously promote others and yourself.* There is a fundamental inconsistency here, and one or the other has to give.

One of the most poignant and piercing examples of the selflessness of Christ was His prayer in the Garden of Gethsemane. While His flesh was screaming "I don't want to do this," His spirit overrode the flesh by humbly submitting the words, "Nevertheless, not my will, but yours, be done" (Luke 22:42).

If you want to know how strong, demanding, and determined the flesh will be to wrestle for its own way, read the narrative of great drops of sweat and blood flowing from Jesus' body as He resisted the flesh while praying at Gethsemane. Everything inside carnal man is driven by selfish motives. There is no better way to deny the flesh than to seek the will of another, beginning with total obedience to God. "Not my will, but yours be done" needs to be the never-ending cry of our hearts and the foundation for all our decisions.

The Apostle Paul began his introduction to the selfless life of Christ by exhorting, "Do nothing from selfish ambition or conceit, but in humility count others more significant than yourselves" (Philippians 2:3).

If this one scripture were followed, it would virtually eliminate most divorces, church splits, political conniving, and broken relationships. It would eliminate most wars as well.

Husbands must prefer their wives above themselves.

Wives must choose to honor their husband's wishes rather than insisting on their own way.

Employees must see the welfare of their employers as more important than seeking their own advancement.

Employers must consider their workers more important than themselves.

Unless selfishness is dealt with, there can be no purity or effectiveness in leadership. Great leaders are giving, generous people, not selfish. I'm confident that if you choose to take this principle to heart, and purpose to lead as Jesus led, you will have dramatic changes in your leadership. This might greatly reduce "selfies," promotional advertising, reserved seating and parking, Facebook posts, exaggerated, bloviated biographical sketches, billboards, and all other signs of self-promotion. Maybe pastors would no longer need to boast about how many attended their services on Easter. It's amazing how many people would follow you if you choose to put the vision and goals of others ahead of your own.

My first ministry was a mixed bag, featuring both top-down, heavy-handed leadership as well as an underlying desire to see people released in their gifts. All I had ever known growing up were leaders who led through coercion, intimidation, posturing, politicking, manipulating, and demanding absolute subservience from those under them.

Although I was never that heavy-handed, I have to admit that I used authority for my own benefit. It never occurred to me that there was a better way; I could lead from the bottom up, allowing the people to be fully released in their callings, and serving them as Jesus served His disciples.

I couldn't think of a single leader I had ever been exposed to who led like Jesus, choosing to do the will of the Father rather than His own pre-determined vision. I had no examples to follow. I had never seen a man lay His life down for the sheep. I had only known those who exploited the sheep for their own gain.

Though there were times when my compassion overpowered my thirst for authority, I'm sure it wasn't the norm. Self was definitely seated on the throne of my life. As I will describe in detail later in the book, there came a time when I climbed off the throne of self-rule and submitted myself entirely to only doing the will of the Father. I will never forget the day I died to self-promotion. I was driving out of town in a U-Haul truck with the only things we still owned in this world. I was crying so hard I could hardly see the road, and I began to pray this prayer: "Lord, I no longer need a big home, a big car, a big church, a big reputation, a big salary, or even authority. All

I need is you. If I have you, I have everything. If I don't have you, I have nothing."

I can truly say that on that day, Larry Titus died, and Jesus began to live in me. I had lost everything so I could gain the only thing that really mattered: Jesus. At last, I was becoming the leader I had so long been looking for. When I died to self, I discovered the joy of leading from the bottom up, not the top down.

The world's greatest leader led from the bottom up, not the top down. I had never seen it lived out by the leaders I had followed, but I decided to follow the only Leader who truly mattered, Jesus of Nazareth.

If you choose to make yourself nothing so that others can be something, you will have then taken the first and most important step in leading like Jesus led.

CHAPTER 2

Lead
by serving

I don't know what your destiny will be, but one thing I know: the only ones among you who will be really happy are those who have sought and found how to serve.

Albert Schweitzer

"Who is more important, the one who sits at the table or the one who serves? The one who sits at the table, of course. But not here! For I am among you as one who serves."

Luke 22:27 NLT

The Father and the Son once made two universe-shattering decisions. One, that God would come to Earth in the human form of His Son. As a man, Jesus would live, preach, and die on a cross for the sins of humanity. Their second decision was of equal importance: when God came in the flesh, He would empty Himself of all privileges of Deity and take on the nature of a servant. He wouldn't wear royal robes or be adorned with kingly jewels and gold. No, He would cinch up a servant's towel around His waist and kneel in the dust and grime, washing dirty feet as an example to us all. I will never comprehend that kind of love. Who could? We can only bow our heads in awe.

We are aware of the massive consequences of the cross, but more thought and attention should be given to the character of Jesus. Jesus did not appear among us as awe-inspiring royalty. He did not choose to come as a superstar or an iconic ruler. Jesus chose to reveal Himself as a servant. Again, we can only sink to our knees in gratitude and humility. Why did He lower Himself to live among us? He was born a long-awaited king, and died an unjustly-accused criminal.

Philippians 2:7 tells us that when Jesus emptied Himself of His equality with the Father, He slipped into the garments of a common servant. As humans, many of us choose to ignore those who serve us. Oftentimes we tend to overlook them, appearing not to care about learning their names, remembering their faces, or coming to know their lives behind the scenes. Sometimes servants are nearly invisible. But Jesus *chose* to be a servant. The towel became His symbol of identification with others who serve mankind. He went from the highest heights to the lowest lows. And, we must not forget, this was *His choice*.

Jesus was born in a stable, a place for animals. The birth announcement was made by the angel to humble shepherds. After Jesus began His ministry, He had no home or rented room in which to lay His head. Going to the cross, He had a single piece of clothing, and even that was stripped from Him. He loved His own people and they despised Him. Men hid their faces from Him. His brothers and sisters rejected Him. Secret disciples buried Him in a borrowed tomb.

Our Lord lived the life of a common servant. Jesus enjoyed no respite from poverty. Unlike an actor, He could not step out of character, retreat, or kick up His feet to relax in lavish comfort. He owned nothing but the clothes on His back. Remember this when you assess people.

History teaches us that valuable people may not display contemporary symbols of money and status, but they have a purpose that far outweighs material goods. As leaders, we are fools if we make decisions about people based on appearance. A true leader sees beyond appearances and looks deeply into people's souls.

As a pastor, I have sat and prayed with the dying countless times, deep into the night after the hospital halls have darkened and at every other time of day. I have never heard people facing death speak of the status or possessions they acquired. On the contrary, they speak of their regrets and happy moments, their families and friends. Please don't value status and possessions as you lead your life. *Look to what Jesus valued and make those things your goals and treasures.*

What Is Your Title?

Have you noticed how people might act when bestowed a little power or recognition? When people receive a new title or a corner office, they often inflate with attitude and ego. They may become remote and unapproachable, unavailable to people they should work hard to know better. Years ago, there was a leadership style known as "Management by Walking Around." The corporate world brimmed with such self-important and isolated leaders that someone had to coin a phrase to encourage managers to wander around the desks and workplaces of their employees. Who wandered and traveled amongst people more than Jesus?

You might have noticed that Jesus didn't embellish His life with a title. The only title officially given Him was "King of the Jews," written on a sign nailed to His cross. Most often, Jesus referred to Himself as the Son of man, indicating His *total identification with mankind.* As we see the life of Jesus in this detail, we understand His utter disdain for titles men give themselves. They meant nothing to Him.

To the Greek mind, a slave (*doulos,* a word used 126 times in the New Testament) referred to ultimate degradation and humility. Since the Greeks' highest value was freedom, their lowest value was servitude. Only the lowest in society were slaves. In fact, soldiers of the time often became slaves when captured by an enemy. Roman and Greek society wouldn't enslave their own; they reserved slavery for those conquered in battle.

To the Greeks, the most dreadful fact of slavery was the loss of free will. A slave always had to do the will of another.

He lost his ability to choose for himself and suffocated as a person. Slavery was worse than abject poverty, because even the poor could make their own decisions.

The decision to come to Earth not as royalty, but as a servant, is what made Jesus exclusively unparalleled and totally different from any leader who ever lived. Review the leaders of the last two millennia. There are a few leaders who assumed physical poverty, like Mahatma Gandhi, but these men had not descended from the place Jesus occupied before coming to live among us.

Jesus Was ...

Let's review the essential facts about Jesus:

- Jesus was the Creator of the Universe and everything in it.
- Jesus was totally divine and totally human in one nature.
- Jesus was unified in relationship with the Father from eternity.
- Jesus descended from unfathomable riches to abject poverty.
- Jesus is the one and only person ever born in the womb of a virgin without an earthly father. He was born of the Holy Spirit.
- Jesus was born to die. His death was self-decreed from eternity. He was not assassinated; He chose the cross.
- Jesus died for the sins of the world, not the independence of a nation.

Jesus Reached for the Servant's Towel

Jesus knew who He was; therefore, He didn't have to prove it. Here is a truism that can puzzle you for the rest of your life. When the Creator of the Universe chose to exchange His robes of royalty and resplendent glory, He reached all the way to the bottom of humanity's wardrobe and retrieved a servant's towel. Couldn't He choose something in-between? Perhaps He could have shopped, not at our exclusive mall stores, but somewhere fitting for those seeking discount bargains. Why did He reach for a servant's cloth?

I suspect that the accessory of choice at the Last Supper was intended to be the ultimate "visual" for all those fighting for prestige and recognition. It was the "show and tell" of all leadership examples. *The World's Greatest Leader led not from above, but from beneath.*

That is why nearly every epistle begins with the words, "A servant of Jesus Christ." If the disciples were going to look like Jesus, they had to glean their identity from service. More importantly, they had to behave like servants. I chuckle and praise God as I write this, for I am remembering a man from one of my earlier churches. He drove a delivery truck. He was one of the greatest evangelists I've ever seen. At every delivery stop the van door would open and a man would bounce out with a smile as big as the sun, and inevitably someone would soon accept Jesus as their savior. I think that if Jesus lived today, He might drive a delivery truck—full of towels, of course.

Let's change the sign on all the parking lots to read: "Reserved for Servants." That would go over well, wouldn't it? Instead of saying, "Reserved for President," "CEO," "CFO,"

"Apostle," or "Pastor," it would read, "Reserved for Servants." But then, you would have to move the sign to the end of the parking lot, the place where servants park.

Other options could include special stationery, titled, "Larry Titus, Servant." Even biographical sketches could carry the moniker, "Servant." But then, who would read it? Maybe that's the point. Jesus didn't give His life on the cross just to make an impression.

Even demons knew how to address Paul and Silas: "These men are servants of the Most High God" (Acts 16:17). Didn't they know they were Apostles?

I love the prayer of the early church in Acts 4. When the disciples asked for boldness to preach accompanied by signs, wonders, and miracles, they prayed in the name of God's *holy servant, Jesus.*

Several motivational speakers have used this anonymous quote: *"If serving is below you, leadership is beyond you."* How true.

Someone recently asked me what my title was. My response was not an attempt to be cute or self-deprecating, but a sincere response of what I consider to be the ultimate title. I said, "I'm just a servant." The person looked at me with a puzzled expression and the unspoken words, "Are you trying to be cute?" No. I honestly believe that we deserve nothing more than the garments Jesus wore.

Who Do You Serve?

I serve my wife. I serve my kids. I serve my friends. I serve pastors. I serve businessmen. I serve the Church. *I love serving. To me it's the purest gold in relationships and the best of leadership paradigms.* There is no greater leadership style than that of serving.

I doubt there would ever be a church conflict if the goal of all its members were to serve Jesus and one another. According to James 3:16, conflicts arise from selfish ambition and jealousy. Servants don't need to be seen, noticed, listened to, applauded, or recognized. After all, servanthood is their identity. Selfish ambition and jealousy don't compete in the servant's heart. *Yet it is the true servants who move and shake our world.*

Years ago, I stood at the window of a hotel on the Mount of Olives, overlooking the valleys and hills of Judea that extend south toward Bethlehem. I could see a shepherd, his flock of sheep grazing quietly beneath my window. I was curious if the shepherd would soon round up his sheep, place them in someone's care or a protective fence, and head off to his nomadic camp for the evening. To my surprise, as the sun was setting, he squatted down in the middle of the flock and put his cloak over his head. That was his bed for the evening. He evidently didn't have an assistant shepherd or vice-president of shepherds to watch the sheep in his absence.

How profound! At the end of the day, all I am is a servant, a shepherd willing to serve the sheep. One man told me he wanted to be part of our congregation because he could smell the scent of sheep on me. I felt honored beyond all words.

Jesus made it clear that Gentiles are always seeking titles and authority so they can rule over someone else, but *in God's kingdom, the greatest will be the least and the last will be the first, and the servant will be greatest of all.* Jesus said:

It shall not be so among you. But whoever would be great among you must be your servant, and whoever would be first among you must be your slave, even as the Son of Man came not to be served but to serve, and to give his life as a ransom for many. (Matthew 20:26-28)

If the Son of Man came to this world to serve people, that should be our goal as well.

How do we make this echo in our daily lives? I can answer that! Let's say someone retrieves your mail. Magically it appears every day on your desk. In the morning, your office is clean and the garbage can empty. These tasks seem to happen all by themselves. True leaders pay attention to these acts of service, and more importantly, true leaders serve back. Sometimes, all that's required is to gratefully acknowledge and recognize the individuals around you. Try it! It works! When you recognize those who serve you, an outpouring of goodness flows from you to them. When people think you really care about them, they are motivated beyond belief. As I like to say, "Let them suspect you love them!"

Jesus Gave His Life as a Ransom

The second purpose of Jesus' coming was to give His life as a ransom. Notice how the two goals merge together. To purchase a slave, you must pay the price. This is the only time in history when a servant purchased slaves. Jesus Christ was the ultimate servant who purchased us with His blood. We have been "bought back" by God, redeemed from slavery to Satan

> # If the Son of Man
> # came to this world
> # to serve people, that
> # should be our goal
> # as well.

so that we may serve our Lord in righteousness. We were all slaves purchased by a servant, the Lord Jesus Christ.

If you want to be a great leader, start looking for the servant's towel, and be ready to bleed in some fashion, for you can only emulate Jesus if you give of your own body as He did.

> Have this mind among yourselves, which is yours in Christ Jesus, who, though he was in the form of God, did not count equality with God a thing to be grasped, but emptied himself, by taking the form of a servant. (Philippians 2:5-7).

I must repeat this. It is too important to miss. When Jesus came to live with us, by our sides, He chose the role of a servant. He didn't go to tailors or purveyors of fine threads to purchase His clothes. He was lowly in appearance and attitude. Though by redemption we are kings with a royal bloodline, by position we are only servants to Jesus and each other.

The mother of James and John brought the topic to the forefront when she asked that her sons have select seats in the kingdom. To her request Jesus responded, "But among you it will be different. Whoever wants to be a leader among you must be your servant, and whoever wants to be first among you must become your slave" (Matthew 20:26-27 NLT).

In my travels, I've encountered many whining, demanding, querulous leaders! It's especially embarrassing in restaurants when they never submit their order to the waitstaff without adding all kinds of extra demands. Then when the food is brought, nothing pleases them. Everything is wrong; the food is too cold or hot, the silverware isn't clean, and everything needs to be returned at least once. Their negative attitude, reflected in a small tip, displays more arrogance than humility. I always hope the waiter didn't see them pray over the food, a dead giveaway that they claim to be Christians. Often in those situations I've slipped an extra tip to the waiter, hoping it will mollify his unpleasant experience with Christian "leaders."

Jesus Washes Our Feet

On Jesus' final night on earth, He took off His outer robe, wrapped Himself with the towel of a common servant, and began to wash his disciples' feet. Nothing could be lowlier. Nothing could have given a more sublime illustration of what it means to serve. To serve dinner at a table or draw water for someone is understandable, but to witness the Master wash someone's feet is unheard of. But Jesus did it. Even the most convinced atheist or agnostic, if they have any intellectual honesty, must read of Jesus' documented act of washing His followers' feet and be astonished and baffled. The daily walk of Jesus is compelling even for those who don't follow Him.

After His show-and-tell, Jesus said, "If I then your Lord and Teacher, have washed your feet, you also ought to wash

I've never known anyone to be offended by being served.

one another's feet. For I have given you an example, that you also should do just as I have done to you. Truly, truly, I say to you, a servant is not greater than his master, nor is a messenger greater than the one who sent him. If you know these things, blessed are you if you do them" (John 13:14-17).

If you know these things and do them, then what? It's too simple. If you take the role of a servant and wash the feet of others, you will have imitated something Jesus did right here on earth. If you do it with the same heart He had, you *will* be blessed!

We have a group that works closely with us called "Feet That Move." It's a shoe distribution ministry led by an incredible young man, Dustin Sandoval. They not only distribute shoes to the poor in developing nations, but they also wash their feet, pray for them, and share the gospel with them. They're imitating Jesus. It's amazing how simply serving people can open hearts for the gospel.

I've never known anyone to be offended by being served. On the other hand, I constantly see the negative results when people attempt to arrogantly lord their authority over others. We see grim examples of this in the military, where newly-minted officers are hungry to give orders. We see it in corporations, church groups, volunteer organizations, and even sibling pecking orders.

We have too many leaders seeking to make everyone else their servants. And you know what? People everywhere are crying and begging for leadership! But aren't we surrounded by leaders? No! Authentic leaders are as rare as precious gold. If people were given leaders who led as Jesus led, there would be no victims of the arrogant and the officious. There would be followers with changed lives—followers who will become leaders who *lead differently*.

The Old Testament attaches the servant designation to Abraham, Isaac, Jacob, Joshua, Moses, David, and scores of others, including pagan kings. The prophecy of Joel 2, also found in Acts 2, makes it very clear that God would pour His Spirit out on both male and female servants. I don't know about you, but I plan on always striving to be a *servant*. That's a title I *do* want.

When God volunteered someone to be tested by Satan's fiery trials, He proffered the suggestion, "Have you considered my servant Job?" (Job 1:8). Wow! Job qualified to be tested because he was a servant. After his life-altering trial, God restored His servant. Job's life and family were restored and his wealth was doubled (Job 42:10-17). What a beautiful picture of eternal rewards for God's servants.

Because I love you, I'll never tire of trying to get this into your hearts. Here are some quick staccato sentences to remember:

- Clothe yourself as a servant, else God will defrock you.
- Kingdom servants qualify to become kings.
- God's highest compliment is to call someone a servant.

- Do not equate earthly symbols of power and wealth with authentic godly leadership. Jesus chose poverty and homelessness over riches and splendor.
- Wash feet by serving people with the heart of Jesus.

Leaders, it's time to stoop down and knot a towel around our waists.

Jesus' final commendation is the one I personally want to receive on Judgment Day: "Well done, good and faithful servant" (Matthew 25:21).

CHAPTER 3

Lead
with prayer

God does nothing except in response to believing prayer.

John Wesley

"One day Jesus told his disciples a story to show that they should always pray and never give up."

Luke 18:1 NLT

Have you ever wondered why Jesus prayed? If you're God, why pray? Who do you pray to, Yourself? If you can do anything, there's no need to pray, right? Some might say Jesus' prayers were redundant or rhetorical. If you can just "speak" the Word, like you did when you created the universe, then prayer is unnecessary. If you know all things, and you're the omniscient God, then why pray?

Well, Jesus didn't seem conflicted. Hardly—for He prayed constantly. Jesus championed prayer. He bathed His ministry with prayer and taught His disciples to do the same thing. Here are just a few verses revealing the prayer life of Jesus:

- "And rising very early in the morning, while it was still dark, he departed and went out to a desolate place, and there he prayed" (Mark 1:35).
- "Now when all the people were baptized, and when Jesus also had been baptized and was praying, the heavens were opened" (Luke 3:21).
- "But he would withdraw to desolate places and pray" (Luke 5:16).
- "In these days he went out to the mountain to pray, and all night he continued in prayer to God" (Luke 6:12).
- "Now it happened that as he was praying alone, the disciples were with him. And he asked them, 'Who do the crowds say that I am?'" (Luke 9:18).
- "Now about eight days after these sayings he took with him Peter and John and James and went up on the mountain to pray. And as he was praying, the appearance of his face was altered, and his clothing became dazzling white" (Luke 9:28-29).

- "I have prayed for you that your faith may not fail" (Luke 22:32).
- "And he withdrew from them about a stone's throw, and knelt down and prayed" (Luke 22:41).
- "And being in an agony he prayed more earnestly; and his sweat became like great drops of blood falling down to the ground" (Luke 22:44).

The entire chapter of John 17 records one of the final prayers of Jesus, known as Jesus' "High Priestly Prayer."

Jesus prayed in the morning, during the day, at night, and on occasion all night long (Luke 6:12; Matthew 14:23).

He also taught others to pray (Matthew 6:5-15; 7:7-11; Luke 11:1-13).

Jesus taught persistence in prayer (Luke 11:11-13; Luke 18:1-8).

He spent His final night on earth interceding in prayer for His disciples (John 17; Luke 22:32).

Why Did Jesus Pray? The Consummate Example

All these references still beg the question, why did Jesus pray?

The answer is found in Philippians 2:5-9. From eternity, Jesus chose to lay aside all the privileges of deity and limit Himself to the human experience. In so doing, He became the consummate example of what believers should do, which is pray.

Jesus had a habit of nonstop prayer.

I can find few things recorded of Jesus in the Gospels that were as consistent as His custom of relentless prayer. One could say that Jesus had a habit of nonstop prayer.

When the baffled disciples asked Jesus why He could cast out demons and they couldn't, His response was simple: "That's easy, I pray and you don't" (Mark 9:29, my paraphrase).

- Jesus taught that prayer unlocks the door to God's limitless storehouse of gifts to flow from the Father to the child (Matthew 7:7-11; Luke 11:1-13).
- Prayer was the method whereby Jesus established and maintained an intimate relationship with the Father (John 17; Luke 22:40-44).
- The Gospels show that prayer was the source of power in the life of Jesus (compare Luke 5:16 with Luke 5:17, and Luke 6:12 with Luke 6:19).
- Prayer was the power that caused Jesus to walk on water while the disciples strove all night to row the few miles to the other side of Galilee (Matthew 14:23-25).
- Prayer for His disciples was the last activity of Jesus in the Garden of Gethsemane before being led to His trial and execution (John 17).
- Jesus described Herod's temple as a "house of prayer." He went even further, possessively calling the house of prayer both His and His Father's. When His Father's

house had become a "den of merchandisers," it drew a speedy and stinging rebuke at the end of a whip (Matthew 21:13; Luke 19:45-46; John 2:16-17).

- Jesus spent the night in prayer before choosing His disciples (Luke 6:12).
- Jesus was in prayer when the Father spoke audibly to Him from heaven (Luke 3:21; John 12:28).
- Jesus prayed on the cross (Matthew 27:46).

So many houses of worship rarely include more than a few perfunctory words of prayer at the beginning, middle, and end of a service. This is tragic! Prayer must be a recognized subtheme of any gathering done in the name of Jesus. Prayer must gently pulse under a church service like a bass note in music. Prayer should be yielded to at any moment directed by the Holy Spirit. I have held services where the Holy Spirit's guidance was simply that of prayer. At times I have set aside my prepared text and we have prayed for the entire scheduled time of the service. Prayer is paramount! We cannot let it be pushed out of our gatherings or our lives.

Today's congregations do not know how to pray. In many cases it has not been modeled for them by their leaders, creating inexperience and uncertainty.

And yet the book and product sales are doing quite well, thank you. We have racks of books and CDs for sale, and often we promote these more than we pray.

If you would become a leader in the fashion of Jesus, you must return to the foundation of prayer. If Jesus were to show up today at some of our churches, He might not be welcome, for some of our churches have become primarily houses for merchandisers and money changers. The whip in Jesus' hand

> ## Through prayer, man's natural becomes God's supernatural.

would be employed just as it was in Jerusalem. He would cleanse such a church and offer no benediction.

Book and DVD resources are an extension of our training, but cannot replace prayer.

Prayer is the only thing I know that allows man to partner with God in fulfilling His will on earth.

- Through prayer, man's *natural* becomes God's *supernatural.*
- When man's finite hand touches the hand of God, it becomes an extension of the infinite.
- History and eternity are both affected through the prayers of the believers.

God can do anything, all by Himself, without the aid of any human intervention. But God is a compassionate God and He wants to conjoin mankind to His ways. God has chosen to bring man into alignment and partnership with His eternal power and purpose through the vehicle of prayer. It might seem as simple and crude as people stretching a string between two tin cans and using their device as a telephone. Why should God need to listen to man? But He does, and He encourages us to pray and bring heaven to earth. We can change the course of history by prayer!

- Prayer is the world's tallest extension ladder. It takes us to heaven and brings heaven to us.
- Prayer is the fuse that ignites the dynamite of God's power inside the believer.
- Prayer transcends time and connects the future with the present.
- Prayer allows the believer to fulfill Jesus' prayer and do on earth what He has already done in heaven (Matthew 6:9, 10).

A great reason to read all the Gospels is that we mine nuggets of truth in one that are missing from others. For example, in Matthew 16:15, Jesus asks Peter the question, *"Who do you say that I am?"* and Peter's famous and oft-quoted response is, *"You are the Christ, the Son of the living God."* I'm thinking, "Good job, Peter. You're a spiritual giant." But there is another aspect to Peter's response. Luke 9:18 records that Peter's answer was during a moment when Jesus had been standing in their midst, praying. To make clear that Peter's answer was more than a hunch, Jesus revealed the fact that it was the Father who had given this revelation to Peter. Matthew 16:17. If Jesus prayed in the midst of His disciples, eliciting a response from both Peter and the Father, how much more should we pray together as groups of believers?

The secret power in Jesus' life was a direct result of prayer. Compare these verses and see if you come to the same conclusion: Mark 1:35-45; Luke 5:16-26; 6:12-19. There is a

> The secret power
> in Jesus' life was
> a direct result of
> prayer.

direct correlation between prayer and power. *Prayer equals power; no prayer equals no power.*

If you were to ask a group of your friends, "How many of you are saved today because someone prayed for you?," I can almost guarantee every hand would go up. But, if that's the case, why then don't we spend more time praying for people to be saved? Prayer is a much more effective evangelistic tool than standing on the street corner with a sandwich board reading "repent or you'll go to hell." Prayer brings the Holy Spirit into our midst, and nothing turns our hearts like the presence of the Holy Spirit as we sense the awesome compassion and power of Jesus.

To His disciples, Jesus promised that He would pray to the Father for the Holy Spirit to come as an advocate and remind us about Him. Even the Holy Spirit's coming was a direct result of Jesus praying (John 14:16).

Please do not skim over this truth! *If we imitate Jesus, we must also pray for the presence of the Holy Spirit to hover and intermingle among us and with us.* Evangelism is sparked and empowered by the Holy Spirit. I would even question the effectiveness of any form of evangelism that is not rooted in prayer.

The story is told of five young college students making their way to London's famed Metropolitan Tabernacle to hear the 19th-century preacher, Charles Haddon Spurgeon. They arrived early in the morning at the still-locked Metropolitan Tabernacle. A man approached them and asked, "Would you like to see the heating apparatus of this church?" Down a flight of stairs and through a hallway he led them, then opened the door of a large room. Seven hundred people were on their knees praying. "That is the heating apparatus of this church," said their guide, Charles Spurgeon.

If we were to ask a group of believers, "How many people have been miraculously healed through prayer?" I'm quite sure the number would be high. So why don't we pray for more people to be healed?

The early Church prayed for healing, signs, and wonders to occur, and God responded by sending an earthquake and filling all of them with the Holy Spirit (Acts 4:29-31). Evidently God likes to answer prayers relating to the salvation and healing of people.

Sadly, some believers have become too sophisticated and jaded to pray for healing and other signs and wonders. Are we blasé and so learned that we discount prayers for healing or other signs and wonders? We must not allow cynical modes of thought to run us off the path of imitating Jesus. So pray, and then pray more, for signs, wonders, and miracles. Pray for healing, physical and emotional. Pray for demonic bondages to be broken.

The ten days the disciples spent in the Upper Room, from the time of Jesus' ascension to the Day of Pentecost, must have been spent in heavy prayer. I can't imagine Jesus sending the Holy Spirit, the most powerful event after the Resurrection, in response to anything other than unrelenting prayer. We know for certain that the disciples in Acts 1:14 were continually devoting themselves to prayer. We also know prayer to be the source of power for the early church after the upper room outpouring (Acts 4:29-31).

I don't know of one major revival in America or the world not born from prayer. Prayer initiates revival and sustains revival. From my knowledge of history, when prayer stops, the revival stops.

In April 2006, I had the privilege of standing in a bedroom of a house at 216 North Bonnie Brae Street in Los Angeles, California. It was in this room, one hundred years earlier, that William J. Seymour, the founder of the global Pentecostal revival, prayed for fifteen hours a day from April 9-14, 1906.

Observers on the outside of the home described seeing something that resembled a pillar of fire above the roof of the house. In fact, so many onlookers crowded the porch of the house to see what was causing the conflagration, the porch broke and fell down. What they were seeing wasn't the work of an arsonist, but the Holy Spirit, appearing in fire as He did on the Day of Pentecost. The prayers of William Seymour had lit the fuse that ignited the global Pentecostal conflagration that began at Azusa Street five days later.

I can attest to the fact that the fire of the Holy Spirit ignited by William Seymour's prayers is still burning one hundred years later. The day I stood in that bedroom in 2006, nearly one hundred years to the day later, my entire body felt electrified. I could feel the presence of the Holy Spirit so strongly that my body tingled with the sensation of the presence of God. The hair stood up on my arms, as it is doing now as I retell the story. *The Holy Spirit is drawn to the prayers of the saints as the Father was drawn to the prayers of Jesus.* I believe angels are also drawn to the place of prayer. Daniel 9 and 10 describe both Daniel's prayer and God's immediate response.

In reading the Gospels, we discover an interesting side note to the prayer life of Jesus. On every occasion Jesus prayed through the night, the disciples slept. There were no exceptions.

Whatever deficiencies the disciples had in their prayer lives during the earthly ministry of Jesus disappeared completely after His resurrection and ascension. The early church prioritized prayer. Before and after the Day of Pentecost, the church got their act together and they prayed and prayed and prayed!

Prayer is present in every single chapter in the Book of Acts, beginning with Chapter One through Chapter Sixteen, with the exception of Chapter 15. The early disciples prayed at all times. When scripture doesn't say they were in prayer, it says they were either on the way to prayer, at the place of prayer, or on their way back from prayer. Prayer was the most important activity of the early church. The early disciples and believers finally caught on. They saw through the life of Jesus that nothing from heaven would occur on earth without prevailing prayer.

The reason why we don't see more people overcome the grip of sin, delivered from demonic control, healed of diseases, or released from paralyzing infirmities, as Jesus made clear, is that we don't pray. Nothing of eternal value will be accomplished on earth without prayer. Paul enjoined that we are to "pray without ceasing," meaning at all times, about all things (1 Thessalonians 5:17).

Elijah was Just Like Us

James 5:17 says that Elijah was a man just like us, but when He prayed, God stopped the heavens for forty-two months, only to reopen them again due to prayer. Elijah's prayers brought fire from heaven, empowered him to outrun the king's chariot, and enabled him to destroy the prophets of Baal. James makes it clear that the prayer of a righteous man is powerful and effective.

It's my conviction, through studying Revelation 5:8 and 8:3, that the cataclysmic activities of the very last days during the Great Tribulation will be released when the prayers of God's people fill up the heavenly prayer vials which are then poured out on the earth.

> And when he had taken the scroll, the four living creatures and the twenty-four elders fell down before the Lamb, each holding a harp, and golden bowls full of incense, which are the prayers of the saints. (Revelation 5:8)

> And another angel came and stood at the altar with a golden censer, and he was given much incense to offer with the prayers of all the saints on the golden altar before the throne, and the smoke of the incense, with the prayers of the saints, rose before God from the hand of the angel. (Revelation 8:3-4)

I love this portion of scripture in Daniel 10:12:

> Fear not, Daniel, for from the first day that you set your heart to understand and humbled yourself before our God,

your words have been heard, and I have come because of your words.

Wouldn't it make sense that for all the supernatural activity that has been released on the earth through the prayers of the church during these centuries since Jesus' absence, our prayers would also usher in His return?

We as leaders in the Body of Christ cannot expect to see revival in our churches, cities, or nations without zealous and ardent prayer. The first Great Awakening that occurred in 18th-century America was a result of prayer. The last Great Awakening will be global and will be a direct result of the praying church.

The Story of Daniel Diaz

In November 2013, one of the most promising young youth leaders I have ever met, Daniel Diaz, was shot through the window of his car while waiting for a red traffic light to turn green on a street in Pomona, California. Daniel was killed by a stranger while taking young people home after a church youth event.

In response to Daniel's murder, David and Donna Diaz, his parents and the pastors of New Beginnings Church in Baldwin Park, California, began to pray. For years the Diaz's and their church have prayed every morning at 5 a.m. They moved the prayer vigils to the place of Daniel's murder. Instead of riots, vandalism, and lootings, prayer meetings sprang up around the clock. City pastors began to come together in unity.

From the time of Daniel's death in November 2013 until the end of 2014, the homicide rate went down a staggering 200%. The local pastors believe the drastic decline in homicides was a direct result of prayer.

David and Donna began to minister to the parents of other murder victims. Love, rather than anger and hatred, became the common expression. The continuing prayers of the family and church are producing a harvest of righteousness.

On January 17, 2017, the day of the defendant's trial, Pastor David Diaz, Donna, and the family arrived at the courthouse armed with fifty prayer intercessors from their church. The rest of the story is nothing short of miraculous. After the defendant pleaded "no contest," they were given permission to play a short video in the courtroom of Daniel preaching. Daniel's sister, Doreen, his brother David, Jr., followed by the parents, David and Donna, all stood up and openly forgave their son's murderer. They also encouraged the young man that his future was not over. God had a plan for him that was yet to be fulfilled. God had called him to preach the message of Jesus and His redemption to the men in prison.

The rest of the story is still being written, carried along on the wings of prayer. I am convinced of one thing, however: God responds to prayer and Daniel's death will not be in vain. Prayer will ensure that revival will come, in some form, at some time. The incense of prayer and worship has been offered and the vials will soon be filled to the point of running over and out into the community. What began as a tragedy will end as a triumph because loving people prayed.

Youngstown, Ohio

In 1995, Devi and I moved to Youngstown, Ohio and began a church in the inner city. At the time, Youngstown was the murder capital of Ohio. We had a murder rate five times greater than other cities our size. We began to pray. A few months later, a newspaper article reported that homicides had inexplicably dropped by a significant percentage.

The Mafia controlled much of our local government, including judges, the sheriff, a former prosecutor, a US Representative, and civil authorities. A year after we began to pray, an FBI sting literally wiped out most vestiges of organized crime in our city. Even the county sheriff was arrested for ties with organized crime.

We must see prayer not only as an obligation, but as a special open line of communication to the Lord. Our prayers should be constant and frequent, offered up with total confidence that God hears us and God honors us. Every believer who prays with persistent fervor will receive the incredible attention of the Father. This is part of the promise we have received, and we must not ignore it. Prayer is for our children, for our women, and for our men. Do not assign prayer to others and then ignore it for yourself. Do not miss your opportunity for time with the Father. He is waiting to hear from you. He is waiting for you to lead your life and lead others as His Son did—in prayer.

CHAPTER 4

Lead
hrough reproduction

Go therefore and make disciples of all nations, baptizing them in the name of the Father and of the Son and of the Holy Spirit, teaching them to observe all that I have commanded you. And behold, I am with you always, to the end of the age.

Matthew 28:19-20

"And he (Jesus) called to him his twelve disciples and gave them authority . . . The names of the twelve apostles are these: first, Simon, who is called Peter, and Andrew his brother; James the son of Zebedee, and John his brother; Philip and Bartholomew; Thomas and Matthew the tax collector; James the son of Alphaeus, and Thaddaeus; Simon the Zealot, and Judas Iscariot, who betrayed him."

Matthew 10:1-4

How does the world typically choose candidates for leadership? Naturally, we look for talented people with impeccable resumes, good grooming habits, charisma, charm, and good breeding.

That's how the world does it. But let's take a close look at how *Jesus* chose leaders, because Jesus' ways are always different.

After praying all night for the Father to give Him wisdom, Jesus selected men who would be at the bottom of most recruiting lists. His choices seemed wildly random and unconventional by worldly standards. Certainly, He picked a team that was the polar opposite of "ideal." I wouldn't call them the scum of ancient Israel, but neither were they the elite of the Palestinian crop.

Only one of them was educated—Judas Iscariot. The others clearly suffered from bad cases of ne'er-do-well syndrome.

- Four were fishermen. After they met Jesus, they left their boats, which was probably good because the Gospels never record them catching any fish unless Jesus was with them.
- Two of them, James and John, were called "Sons of Thunder," a description alluding to their out-of-control temperament.
- Matthew worked for the Roman version of the IRS.
- Thomas was the quintessential pessimist and doubter. He was a twin, which begs the question what his brother was like. Would he have been a better choice?
- One, Nathaniel, disparaged Jesus before he even met Him, asking the famous question, "Can anything good

come from Nazareth?" He was judgmental and maybe even racist.

- Another was a radical revolutionary and anarchist, barely one step ahead of the law. Insurrection was his game and he played it well. His name, Simon the Zealot, gave it away.
- James, the son of Alphaeus, had the unfortunate epithet of being "the Less." That's a setup for an inferiority complex. Why didn't his parents name him "James the More?" Who wants to be "James the Less?"
- Eleven of the twelve men who followed Jesus were Galileans. Most Galileans received no real education. Even Luke, in the Book of Acts, refers to that fact (Acts 4:13).
- By the world's standards, Judas Iscariot was the one in the group with the right stuff, a CPA from the Jerusalem precincts, an educated man. Jesus trusted him with the treasury. In the beginning, Judas appeared to be the one with potential for success in the group. All the others, by appearances, were doomed to remain in the dust-heaps of forgotten men. They seemed destined for insignificance and anonymity; no one would be willing to invest in them. They were identified by that horrible distinction of being "common."

Despite their apparent commonness, Jesus called them and they left everything—their families, their possessions, their livelihoods, to follow Him, a person they barely knew. If it were not for Jesus, the master disciple-maker, Peter, James, and John would not be household names today in nearly every language on earth. If it were not for Jesus, they would have remained

Good teachers can turn mediocre people into extraordinary people.

unremarkable and passed over by history. But because Jesus saw something extraordinary in them, they changed the world.

Jesus showed us that through discipleship, good leaders are able to take common men with apparently small potential and make them great leaders. *It's the quality of the leader, not the quality of the disciple, that makes the difference.*

This has caused a fire to burn in me all my life. It is something the Holy Spirit showed me early on and used to direct my steps, my days, and my years as a leader. This is a truth that rings like a bell and sparks joy and hope in me.

Turning Ordinary into Extraordinary

The truth is that good leaders, good coaches, and good teachers can turn mediocre people into extraordinary people. It's true! It's powerful. It is a divine concept enabled by the Holy Spirit and given to His people.

I have seen devoted and passionate coaches make great players out of undisciplined, mediocre talent. I have seen gifted orchestra directors make awesome orchestras out of ordinary musicians. I have witnessed extraordinary teachers make outstanding students out of under-performing children. Committed leaders and teachers, using discipleship principles, can make world-changers out of ordinary people.

Jesus took twelve nobodies, and, with the exception of Judas who betrayed Him, made eleven of them world-changers. This band of motley, under-performing Galileans turned the world upside down within two decades of Jesus' resurrection.

Discipleship is not only a principle of Christian leadership; it's a principle of all leadership. The question is not so much how good the student is; it's really how much the inspired leader is willing to pour into the student.

Discipleship makes the difference. It is at the heart of leadership training. In the working world, there is a training process where one person is the mentor and the other is the intern. Labor unions call the mentor the "master" and the intern the "apprentice." Medical doctors "intern" before they can begin their own practice. This model has been used since Socrates. For centuries, budding artists moved in with their masters until they became great artists—their mediocrity became extraordinary.

Discipleship is, "Watch me, see what I do, and then do it."

Discipleship is not, "Listen to what I say and do it." The Apostle Paul put it succinctly in 1 Corinthians 11:1: "Be imitators of me, as I am of Christ." The Greek word for "imitate" is *mimetes*, from which we derive our word "mimic." The principle is follow me, as I follow Christ. When I step, you step. Follow me as long as the Lord puts you with me, and then do the same for those who are following you. Ultimately there will come a time in the life of each disciple when he will no longer follow, but will lead.

Discipleship is not learned in a classroom. Classes cannot provide in-depth, hands-on, real-life training. Even the best classes rarely feature more than a lecture. In a classroom, deep relationships are not formed between teacher and student. The student cannot see the teacher's family life, his daily interactions with people, or the course of his day, lived hour-by-hour. In the academic setting, the student has no way to participate in the mentor's daily life.

Jesus did quite the opposite; He asked His students to follow Him and see His life. Jesus' classroom was on the road. For three and a half years, they trailed Him around 24/7 and soaked up the essence of what He did and said. He became transparent to them and let them experience every detail of His life. He allowed them to watch, follow, glean, observe, see, imitate, and question. They didn't read a book. The disciples walked the roads, talked with Jesus, and witnessed miracles.

The personal impact Jesus had on the disciples is easily seen in the First Epistle of John.

The beloved Apostle begins his letter with a personal description of their experience with the Master: "We proclaim to you the one who existed from the beginning, whom we have heard and seen. We saw him with our own eyes and touched him with our own hands. He is the Word of life. This one who is life itself was revealed to us, and we have seen him" (1 John 1:1-2 NLT).

Could anything be more personal? Much of our current discipleship practices are anything but hands-on. What a far cry from many modern preachers, whose disciples will rarely get the chance to either see them personally or touch them.

Rather than teach them, Jesus *showed* them. They saw His reaction to every situation. Rather than lecture them, He

> A true mentor will
> engage all five
> senses.

walked and held conversations with them. The Word became living and apparent to them. This points to an absolutely necessary principle of successful discipleship: you must *show* and not *just tell* those you disciple. You must let your actions speak even louder than your words.

Recently, a young leader from Brazil stayed in my home for ten days. Just before he left, I asked him to review the time we'd had together. I asked him what his most memorable experience was during the trip. I thought he'd name one of the tourist spots we visited, maybe a restaurant we'd eaten in, or someone I had introduced him to. I was sure that the visit to the AT&T Stadium, where the Dallas Cowboys play, would be the highlight of the tourist hotspots we covered. If not, then seeing real cowboys steering a cattle drive in historic Fort Worth would rank high on his list.

I was wrong.

His answer was telling. "Watching you and Devi was the most special memory for me: what you did, how you treated each other, how you loved each other, how you interacted with each other, and even how you got up from the table and cleaned the dishes. You answered all your calls, emails, and texts immediately. I've never known a leader to do that. I read your book, *The Teleios Man*, but this was even better. I saw what you did."

A True Mentor Is Touchable

A true mentor will engage all five senses. Their mentee will learn from what they see, feel, hear, smell, and touch.

What do you think impacted the disciples most: Jesus' sermons or His actions; His miracles or His companionship? Think about it! An equally important question is, what would people see or hear or how would they feel if they spent ten days with you?

Every mom and dad must use discipleship principles, or their children will grow up without any form of character training. The lack of discipleship in a child produces carelessness, rebellion, indolence, impudence, laziness, and disrespect. Ignore discipleship training in your son or daughter, and you risk forming a child undefended from depression and other mood disorders, drug use, sexual license, and all the other traps that snare our kids. An undisciplined child won't have the structure and boundaries needed to contain his own personality. That child will be vulnerable and damaged.

Parents who bark out orders to their children without lovingly showing them by example risk raising a child trapped in a lifetime of alienation, disobedience, and perpetual immaturity. We must teach by example or we travel a slippery slope with our child.

It is only fitting and right that Jesus' final words express what He Himself had been doing for three and a half years. Matthew 28:19 records Jesus standing on the Mount of Olives declaring, "Go therefore and make disciples of all nations." It is a fact that Jesus spent the majority of His time training the twelve men whom He chose to have a relationship with, rather than only preaching to the multitudes.

Of course, Jesus did preach to the multitudes—especially during the Sermon on the Mount, the feeding of the five thousand, and His final week in Jerusalem. But He spent 24 hours a day, seven days a week, 365 days a year, training twelve men. He even ate His meals with them. I wonder how many leaders would commit to that regimen today?

Shortly after Devi and I became pastors of a church in Camp Hill, Pennsylvania, I began to disciple Gene McGuire, an inmate with a life sentence who I had met at a series of revival meetings inside the prison chapel. That discipleship continued for twenty-five years until Gene was finally released from his life sentence on April 3, 2012. For twenty-five years, every birthday, Christmas, and Thanksgiving, my family would find me behind bars discipling Gene. For the first several years I was able to go into the prison on a weekly basis. After we moved to Ohio, my visits were reduced to a monthly visit requiring a 6-hour drive. I not only went in by myself, but I took my family, friends, church members, and even my aged mother into the prison to see Gene. When people would come to visit us on a vacation, I'd take them in too. Gene was like part of my tour itinerary. "Would you like to visit the NFL Football Hall of Fame in Canton? Would you like to go to a baseball game in Cleveland? Would you like to go visit Gene McGuire at a prison in Bellefonte, Pennsylvania?" I believe in sticking with a person for the long haul.

By the way, Gene McGuire now has his own book, *Unshackled*. How can a man serve thirty-five years in prison for a crime he didn't commit and come out without a hint of bitterness? But Gene did, and his book tells you how. It is actually far more than an autobiography; it's one of the greatest discipleship books I've ever read. You must order it online today. Right now.

Why don't we disciple others the way Jesus did? Why don't we pull people into the very minutes and seconds of our lives? Why don't we eat our meals, do our errands, and pray openly with those we lead?

Discipleship is a concept mostly foreign to the Old Testament. Moses had his assistant, and Elisha stubbornly followed Elijah around wherever he went, but they never mentored them like Jesus did. The revelation of discipleship as God's way of training leaders and believers wouldn't be fully shown to us until Jesus was here in an earthly form and walked with His twelve disciples. He taught a new way of leading; Jesus led differently.

Watch Me!

Discipleship entails more than teaching; it shows people by example what they are to do. It allows them into your life. It permits them to walk with you and observe how you lead. It lets them see your character. It invites them to share in your authority. It allows them to even see your weaknesses, a valuable part of their training. By being attentive to your mistakes, they can avoid pitfalls and gain wisdom. They should feel loved, affirmed, confident, and set free to copy their leader's example. Discipleship blows wind into their sails. Discipleship confirms their call and validates their anointing.

Many leaders are afraid of discipleship because it requires vulnerability and transparency, but vulnerability is the key to connection. It's impossible to keep your followers at a distance and disciple them at the same time. Either you allow them to observe you first-hand or you abdicate your responsibility as a spiritual father or mother.

In the Greek era before Christ, a father who didn't want to be bothered to train his own children would hire teachers to walk along with them to school and teach them. They were called pedagogues (*paidagogos*), paid teachers.

Paul points out to the Corinthian church (1 Corinthians 4:14-17) that there are thousands of paid teachers among them who are willing to receive money for their services, but are unwilling to be fathers. "Though you have countless guides [*paidogogos*] in Christ, you do not have many fathers. For I became your father in Christ Jesus through the gospel" (1 Corinthians 4:15). It is impossible to be a father in the faith yet refuse to invest in the lives of your disciples. Discipleship is a *hands-on* responsibility, not something you can *hand off* to paid teachers. If you're unwilling to do the "dirty work" of discipleship, you're unqualified to be a father in the faith. The heart of God, profoundly revealed by Jesus, is to enter into a mentoring, fatherly relationship, rather than to hire teachers.

Through the years, I've taken hundreds of men with me on speaking or mission trips for the purpose of training them how to pray, how to study the Word of God, how to minister to people, how to discover God's purpose in their lives, and how to relationally treat their wives. Long road trips are excellent for such training purposes. They become a captive audience. Even doing yard or church work together can serve the same purpose. Rather than go by yourself, invite someone along who you want to invest in. You never know—one encounter could change their life forever.

Jesus' final words on this earth were, "Go therefore and make disciples . . ." (Matthew 28:19). He didn't say to make believers, church members, Christians, or good people, but *disciples*. He told His disciples to "Follow me," not, "Listen to me as I preach to the multitudes," or "Sit in my discipleship class." Jesus modeled what it was like to be a disciple, and then told them to do as He did. More importantly, He showed them who the Father was.

Dallas Willard, the late professor of philosophy at University of Southern California in Los Angeles, calls this verse in Matthew 28:19 the "Great Omission," because very few people actually do it. He wrote: "And this is the Great Omission from the Great Commission in which the Great Disparity is firmly rooted. As long as the Great Omission is permitted or sustained, the Great Disparity will flourish."

The Greek word for "countless" in the English Standard Version is generally translated as "ten thousand" in most other versions. The Greek word is *murios*, where we get our English word "myriad." That is what Willard calls "the Great Disparity." We have ten thousand paid teachers, but not many fathers. There is a *Great Disparity*, a big difference between *countless*, meaning tens of thousands, and *not many*. Many are willing to teach, but few are willing to make disciples. Many leaders are willing to preach to the crowds, but disdain discipling the few. When teaching pastors or leaders, I say it this way: you're willing to preach to the crowds on Sunday morning, but unwilling to have coffee with a disciple on Monday morning. Something must change.

Steps of Discipleship

The three steps of discipleship, as modeled by Jesus, are:

1. Be a disciple yourself (Luke 2:49-52).
2. Make or train disciples (Matthew 4:19; 10:1-15).
3. Commission or release disciples to make other disciples (Matthew 28:19-20).

Every leader should make these three steps part of his life. I am a disciple, meaning I am teachable and I am correctable. I have learned discipleship under the authority of a mentor. Second, I will disciple others in the ways of Christ. I will teach them, walk with them, mentor them, and be an example of Christ-likeness. Finally, I will release my disciples to become disciple-makers.

I've devoted one entire chapter in the book to this last step alone (see Chapter 6). Quite often, even those who are good disciple-makers find it difficult to release their disciples. The whole purpose of discipleship is to see men and women released in their calling to make disciples, not to retain them. A good mentor will look forward to the time when his disciples are more successful than he is.

Final Thought

A leader's time would be significantly more effective if they spent more time training the few disciples who God gave them and a bit less time teaching crowds. By doing so, they could develop a core group of powerful disciples and see exponential growth from their ministries. Indeed, they could eventually reach the entire world. You train twelve, and they train twelve, and they train twelve, and within three years the entire world could be reached. Only preaching to assemblages and crowds will not do that.

Imagine making an investment in the financial markets. You typically always know how the investment is doing. You can track your portfolio and see how each stock or bond is performing. But not so with discipleship! You can invest weeks, months, or years in someone and not know how they'll perform until much later. Because discipleship is deeply relational, sometimes it's years before results become evident. If Jesus had a personality prone to depression, the final night before His crucifixion would have been disastrous. One of His disciples betrayed Him; eleven fled when He was arrested; Peter denied Him, not once, but three times. If you're doing the math, you know things weren't looking good. As a leader, nothing could be more depressing than having your followers turn away from you.

Discipleship is like parenting. You may not know the result of your investment for quite a while. Your child will have to become an adult. Your disciples will do some floundering and maturing as they test what you've taught them. It may take years to see a return on your investment. But remember, God's timing is different from ours.

If I were Jesus, I would have felt like a failure. After spending more than three years with His disciples, every one of them denied Him in some way. Can you imagine His thoughts? Or maybe, mine? I might have said to myself, *"What a waste of time. I spent every waking moment with my disciples, and I don't have anything to show for my efforts. Not one of them stuck with me during my hour of trial."*

Long ago, I heard someone wisely say, "Don't count your score at half-time."

In the garden, the disciples openly rejected Him.

At the cross, things were dismal, with only one disciple, John the Beloved, lingering.

After the cross, they all returned to their former way of life in Galilee.

Thankfully, they did show up at the Mount of Olives to say goodbye to their leader and to witness the ascension.

But from the Day of Pentecost on, they moved in power.

It was said of them, "These men who have turned the world upside down have come here also" (Acts 17:6).

The work of world evangelism that brought the Roman Empire to its knees within four centuries is a testimony to the effectiveness of the disciples, but more profoundly to the effectiveness of Christ as the greatest leader the world has ever known.

With the exception of John the Beloved, every one of the eleven disciples would follow the steps of their leader and die a martyr's death. Do you know why they were willing to die for their leader? Because their leader died for them.

I want to be one of those leaders who loves, trains, exemplifies, and walks the walk until those following me catch it. I want to turn the world upside down, one disciple at a time. In the course of a lifetime of ministry, it's amazing how many you can influence.

In short, I want to lead like Jesus. He *led differently.*

CHAPTER 5

Lead
by mining the gold in people

When we treat man as he is, we make him worse than he is; when we treat him as if he already were what he potentially could be, we make him what he should be.

Goethe

"Looking intently at Simon, Jesus said, 'Your name is Simon, son of John—but you will be called Cephas' (which means 'Peter')."

John 1:42 NLT

Jesus was a gold-digger!

He found gold in places where no one else mined. He could look out over the landscape and see the glint of precious nuggets buried in the mud and mire. Others looked at people and saw useless dirt, but Jesus looked with different eyes and spotted gold. When He saw gold, He freed it from the muck and began refining and polishing it.

That's how Jesus found His disciples. *Where others saw useless dirt, Jesus saw gold.*

Professional baseball teams send out armies of scouts to watch players who might have potential. These scouts have an uncanny ability to look in the small town or obscure place where a kid plays baseball and envision him on a big-league diamond. A baseball scout can go into a town where the locals play on a ragged and patchy field and see that "wow factor" in a player who is meant for bigger and greater things. How do they do it? How did Jesus do it? How should we do it?

Shifting Your Gaze

For some reason it's human nature to see the bad in people before seeing their value. Maybe it's the need to feel superior to others. If we expose the faults of others, our thinking goes, people are more likely to see our strengths. But this perspective has the opposite effect. When you put others down, you degrade yourself. The reverse is also true: when you elevate others, you upgrade yourself! But heads-up here! It takes confidence and faith to lift other people up. You can be a godly, seasoned leader who happily gives up your own thunder by hoisting others above your head. God will bless that sacrifice of preferring others above yourself. When you do this, God will place you higher.

Seeing Saints in Sinners

Jesus had the ability to look at sinners and dream of saints. He looked beyond someone's current state and saw what he or she could become. Then He joyfully deposited worth and purpose into people, and they became what God wanted them to be.

Without exception, the twelve disciples looked more like dross than gold. If I were in Jesus' shoes, attempting to train leaders who could carry on my work, I would have looked in other places. I would have gone where the gold mining was hot. I would have scoured the universities and places where high-achievers gathered. But not so for Jesus. He chose men who were the least promising. By compassionately teaching and polishing these men, something remarkable began to happen. As Jesus walked with them, they slowly absorbed the very character and attributes of Jesus.

It takes a great leader to invest in "nobodies" and make them "somebodies." It takes someone who knows how to dig for gold. It takes staying power, patience, and passion to shovel through the muck and uncover the raw, unshaped person God has gifted with a talent or ministry heretofore uncovered. It is the job of the leader to draw out the precious metal of those he leads. But first, he must believe they have value.

We need more leaders who are willing to put their arms and shoulders into the work and dig for raw gold. It's easy to go to a jewelry counter and purchase refined gold. Any mall

Jesus had the ability to look at sinners and dream of saints.

or main street has places to buy it. But when you select gold that has been mined and worked by others, do you ever ask yourself, "How pure is this metal? What am I really getting? I have put no effort into the purification and production of this gold. What do I have here?"

The process of mining raw metal, refining it, and removing impurities is not an easy one, and it takes a skilled worker to produce pure gold. Likewise, this is not the work of an ungifted or run-of-the-mill leader; it is the true, godly leader who knows how to bring out the best from the seemingly ordinary person.

Greater Works than These Shall You Do

Many leaders fail at the task of finding and polishing gifted people because they're afraid of dimming their own luster. Their own insecurities make them fear that someone might shine more than they do, or end up with more authority, or become greater in recognition and ministry. They're afraid to take the attitude of John the Baptist, who decreased so that Jesus might increase (John 3:30).

God deliver us from this debilitating insecurity!

The greatest legacy a leader can have is disciples more prominent and powerful than himself. Nothing makes me happier than sitting and listening to someone God allowed me to raise up in ministry. I have sat in congregations, smiling from ear to ear, as I watch a spiritual son or daughter minister to others. Do you want recognition in your life as a leader? Then release those you have discipled to do the works that God has called them to. While they might have some of your mannerisms or figures of speech, the greatest thing is their hearts burning with passion for Jesus, just like yours did when you met them and began the process of teaching them.

Jesus was not ignorant of this principle. That's why He said in John 14:12: "Whoever believes in me . . . greater works than these will he do." Can you believe that? Jesus wanted His disciples to do greater works than He did. Who has ever heard of that? What leader dreams of producing men and women who excel them in fruitfulness and productivity? A leader who follows Jesus' way of raising up his disciples will take great joy as his students do greater things!

Give Them a New Name

Let's consider another technique God used. If you carefully trace through biblical examples, you'll see several illustrations of how God changed people's names to identify and reflect their future status.

God changed Abraham's name from "Abram," which means "exalted father," to "Abraham," which means "father of a multitude," thereby enlarging his territory and influence. When God changed Abraham's name, He expanded his inheritance to include blessing the world (Genesis 17:5).

Jacob's name was changed by God from meaning "one who deceives" to Israel, meaning, "He strives with God" (Genesis 32:28).

On Jesus' first encounter with Simon, whose name means, "God has heard," He changed his name to Peter, or Cephas. Peter is from the Greek word *petros*, meaning rock (John 1:42). In Jesus' lifetime, Peter would qualify more as a rock of offense than a rock of stability, but after Jesus' resurrection, he became a pillar in the Church, leading three thousand to Christ at his first sermon. He went on to write two epistles and was a driving force in the establishment of a thriving Church in Judea. Paul even calls him the apostle to the Jews (Galatians 2:8). Jesus saw what Peter could become rather than what he was, thereby releasing his destiny.

Now let's talk about affirmation. This next concept is massively powerful.

The Power of Affirmation

Of all the disciples, only Peter attempted to get out of the boat to walk on water to Jesus (Matthew 14:28-31). What made Peter step out of a safe vessel and onto the water? Well, with a leader like Jesus believing in you, *you* might be able to walk on water. Here's the key for leaders. There is an astonishing power associated with the act of giving affirmation.

Affirmation is the closest thing to a magic bullet in leadership. If you champion someone, if you give them permission to do something, and if you believe in them, they take on the power of a nuclear reactor. I'm not kidding you or overemphasizing this! Jesus permissioned Peter to walk on water, and Peter did

> # Affirmation is the closest thing to a magic bullet in leadership.

it. What happened? It's simple; Peter piggybacked on Jesus' faith and power. Spiritually, he climbed onto Jesus' shoulders and caught the miracle of belief. He strode across the water, no doubt keeping eye contact with Jesus, drawn by the absolute affirmation he saw coming from the One who believed in him.

In your toolbox of leadership techniques, keep affirmation in sight and within reach. Affirmation is a potent gift. It releases us to become all God says we can be.

But the opposite is also true: it's hard to do great things with no one believing in you.

Everywhere Jesus looked, He saw potential in people. He knew how to take "nobodies" and make them "somebodies." He saw success in folks when others saw failure. He ignored the condemnations and judgments put on people and saw their potential and value. He knew how to take non-descript men and women and set them on the road to greatness.

Depositing Worth in Women

Consider the story of the woman who anointed Jesus for burial. Before His death, a woman humbly poured precious perfume on Jesus' head as He reclined at a table. When Judas accused her of wasting money that could have been given to the poor, Jesus defended her, saying, "Why do you trouble the woman? For she has done a beautiful thing to me . . . In pouring this ointment on my body, she has done it to prepare me for burial. Truly, I say to you, wherever this gospel is proclaimed in the whole world, what she has done will also be told in memory of her" (Matthew 26:10, 12-13). Instead of judging her, Jesus looked beyond the surface to her heart and proclaimed her beauty, dignity, and purpose. In so doing, He affirmed her value and granted her a legacy of *eternal worth*. This woman lived two thousand years ago, but the world continues to talk about her.

Likewise, Mary from Magdala, a woman whom Jesus delivered from seven demons, was the first one to be introduced to the resurrected Christ. Before meeting Jesus, Mary was wracked with confusion and pain, but He saw beyond her infirmity and considered her worthy of His healing touch. She followed Him, supporting the disciples out of her own means, from Galilee to the Cross and then to the Tomb where He was buried. When the risen Christ saw her, He said her name, "*Mary*," and charged her to announce His resurrection to the disciples, thereby granting her the honor of becoming the very first mouthpiece of the Gospel (John 20:16-18). Jesus can take a demon-possessed woman and make her famous for healing, testimony, and revelation.

If, as statistics show, seven out of ten women in the world have been abused by men, it is incumbent upon men to heal them. Healing is not possible until we men bring out their greatness by healing words. I've seen many women delivered from their commonness and brokenness by the affirming words of their husbands. Their husbands literally released their greatness. Conversely, I've seen the most talented women beaten down until they were incapable of displaying their significance. You might as well have posted a sign on their foreheads, reading, "I used to be great until my husband got ahold of me."

Men, if you don't promote your wife's greatness, the devil will ensure her failure—and yours as well.

Finding Greatness in Commonness

Are you willing to find greatness in commonness, diamonds in coal, and world-changers in broken men and women? Can you find value in people others see as ordinary? If you are willing, God can use you to release people into their full potential. There is no greater calling!

I've seen so many people who continually talk down to others. "You'll never succeed." "You're just not cut out for greatness." "You just don't have what it takes to go to college." "You'll never be great." These negative-talking people will never unearth diamonds or spot flecks of gold in people. All they see is dirt. What a shame. They have an ability to pick up a spade, like the rest of us, and turn over the sod to reveal hidden gems.

The list of "You'll Never's" is endless. What are parents thinking when they curse their own children with trash talk of never being able to make it? "You're not smart enough, talented enough, good-looking." Who are the parents kidding? If they're made in the image of God, there's no limit to what your students, children, and disciples can do, especially if you encourage them.

Can you find value in people others see as ordinary?

The book *The Jewish Phenomenon,* by Steven Silbiger, gives an illustration of the Jewish mother who introduced her two children, not by their names, but by what they would become: "The doctor is three," the mother answered, "and the lawyer is two." I have no doubt that those two children more than fulfilled their mother's possibility words. Whether they actually became a doctor or lawyer, they knew by her words that they had no limits.

Silbiger goes on to say that while Jewish people make up only two percent of the total US population, they comprise:

- 45% of the top forty of the Forbes 400 richest Americans.
- One-third of multimillionaires.
- 20% of professors at leading universities.
- 40% of partners in the leading New York and Washington, D.C., law firms.
- 25% of all American Nobel Prize winners.

We must ask ourselves why. Is it because they have a mother introducing them as "Doctor" at age three and "Lawyer" at age two, and a dad who believes his sons and daughters should settle for nothing less than the best?

Two thousand years ago, the consummate Jewish disciple-maker left an example for us to follow. If you believe in people, they will rise to their potential. *If you want people to become great, you must recognize their greatness in advance or they will never get there. You must affirm them!*

It doesn't take a genius to look at what Billy Graham became and declare him successful. But in Los Angeles, in 1949, the struggling evangelist had preached for three weeks in a big tent without any visible success. A newspaper magnate by the name of William Randolph Hearst wrote a two-word directive to his staff: "Puff Graham" (meaning, promote him in the press). The rest is history. Over three million people have responded to Graham's invitation to accept Jesus as their Savior, and more than 2.2 billion people worldwide have heard him preach.

I'm sure William Randolph Hearst had little idea of how his simple order to "Puff Graham" would change the world. Although the two men never met, I'm convinced that some of Billy Graham's success must be attributed to Hearst. With a simple affirmation, that little kid from rural Charlotte, North Carolina shook the world with the message of Jesus Christ. Even Billy Graham needed someone to believe in him.

Let me give you an opposite illustration. Wikipedia records the sad story of Prince Edward VIII, who served as King of England for less than a year when he abdicated the throne in 1936 to marry an American woman. Perhaps his short-lived monarchy could be explained by the lack of affirmation given to him by his father, King George V. "After I am dead," George said, "the boy will ruin himself in twelve months." It happened exactly as the father predicted. Was it the father's fault, or was Prince Edward a victim of his own bad choices? Everyone is obviously responsible for their own decisions, but the lack of affirmation from parents can have devastating effects on the future of their children. Without parental support, they can easily give up.

I'm glad my parents never prophesied that about me. The father's prediction came true, but it didn't have to. He could have seen the gold in his son and set him up for success. It was in Prince Edward's DNA to be great, but his father destroyed the seed.

Devi and I recently watched the movie, *I Tonya*, depicting the tragic childhood of one of the world's greatest skaters. For some reason I didn't notice the "R" rating given to the movie or Devi and I would not have chosen to see it. I came away, however, not as much grieved by the abundance of expletives, but by the nagging question of what Tonya Harding could have become had she not been beaten down by her mother and men her entire life. It's a wonder she ever won any championship. My heart goes out to all the Tonyas and Edwards of the world.

Several years ago, there was a young man who began attending our church because he was interested in one of our young women. He was really special, really outstanding. I asked him one day, "You're obviously so outstanding. You must have had awesome parents?"

"Quite the contrary," he replied. "My mother died when I was quite young. My dad was emotionally unstable and put in a mental institution shortly after her death. My two sisters were taken away and we were all put in foster homes. I grew up in foster homes."

"How did you become so outstanding?" I asked.

Just remember that gold is always hidden in the dross.

"I had a football coach who believed in me. That was all I needed. He saw my potential. Because he believed in me, I decided I could accomplish anything."

And he did. In his mid-twenties he had already earned his bachelor's degree, was working on his MBA, and had a pilot's license. Furthermore, he was about to take a beautiful young lady in our church as his bride, with my blessings.

One affirmation. One word of encouragement. One coach who believed in him, and more importantly, told him of his belief.

Coaches, teachers, leaders, pastors, parents: you have an unbelievable opportunity to spot and release potential in people. Just remember that gold is always hidden in the dross.

I recently went to a different hair stylist. His first question to me was a usual one. "So, what do you do?" "I'm a gold digger," I replied. He was shocked and didn't quite know what to say—I certainly didn't look like the typical gold miner. I explained, "I mine gold in people." He is my new field and his soil is rich with potential.

So, leaders, lead differently. Rather than spending all your energy on promoting yourself, look for the gold reserve hidden in other people, and promote them. Are you ready to roll up your sleeves and start digging?

CHAPTER 6

Lead
by delegating
authority

*Authority was meant to be
given away or it becomes
dictatorial.*

Larry Titus

*"I have been given all authority in heaven and on earth.
Therefore, go and make disciples of all the nations."*

Matthew 18:18-19a NLT

Authority is fascinating and powerful. It can be used to bring horrible misery and destruction or it can be used to beget abundance, hope, and prosperity.

Merriam Webster's Dictionary defines authority as "A power to influence or command thought, opinion, or behavior." It may also refer to a person or government who is in command.

Authority can be used destructively or constructively. Depending on who has the authority and how that person implements it, people will heal and flourish or wither and die. It is that simple.

Power illuminates the heart of its holder. My contention is that you really don't know a person until you give him or her authority or money. Since money can be used as a source of power, I can distill my definition even further; you don't really know a person until you give him *authority*, period.

It is impossible to calculate the massive destruction of life and property in the world since man began to control people through authority. While writing this chapter, I read the book *Killing Patton*, by Bill O'Reilly and Martin Dugard. The book chronicles the story of millions of people whose lives were snuffed out by only two of these power-driven madmen, Adolph Hitler and Joseph Stalin. To this list could be added the names of post-war dictators, Pol Pot of Cambodia, Chairman Mao of China, and Ho Chi Minh of Vietnam; the numbers of casualties become staggering. They all had one thing in common: they all used authority to kill, destroy, suppress, manipulate, and annihilate their enemies.

Dating back to the earliest known records, human history is filled with the horrifying chronicles of despotic rulers who were in fact little more than mass murderers. These records clearly demonstrate that humans are capable of abusing power to kill one another.

Search the history of Africa over the past century, or South America, or Asia. See if you can come up with a charitable leader who chose to build his nation rather than stuff his own pockets. They are few and far between. These leaders gained power and used it in some of the worst ways imaginable. How many benevolent governments can you find in the Arab world, where power is held by a few? Can you name a Communist leader who hasn't systematically eliminated most of his enemies, and in some cases, millions of his own people? To this list we could add popes, presidents, kings, cult leaders, denominational leaders, military generals, corporate leaders, school administrators, and a host of other leaders, who were intent on using power to crush their opposition, though maybe not to the same degree.

Every cult is built upon a misuse of authority. In November 1978, Jim Jones led nearly a thousand people to their deaths in Jonestown, Guyana, using his dynamic personality to first inspire, pretend to liberate, then suppress and kill those he led. The same is true with many, if not the majority, of despotic leaders around the globe. Who benefited from their dictatorial edicts? Only their closest friends, families, or allies accrued any of this ill-gotten gain.

By the way, you can kill people in many ways besides spiking their punch with cyanide. You can keep them suppressed for decades and kill them slowly, like death by a thousand cuts, rather than murder them immediately. Poverty and hopelessness kill just as surely as the AK-47 or poisonous gas.

Every evil government is built on the negative authority of the leader. Hitler, Stalin, Pol Pot, and Mao Zedong used power

Every cult is built upon a misuse of authority.

to smother the hearts of the people and terrorize them with atrocious acts of torture and death. My brain cannot fathom the depth of evil displayed by so many leaders who committed the atrocities of the Holocaust, led by Hitler, when the lives of six million Jews were snuffed out.

In ancient times, ruthless leaders destroyed hundreds of thousands of people, all because they had the authority to do so. Attila the Hun looks like a Sunday school teacher compared with other evil leaders from antiquity up to the current time.

In biblical days, Saul chased David around the wilderness for years, abusing his authority over David, who was actually the superior leader. It's always that way. Small leaders, large in their own minds, try to suppress upcoming leaders who have great potential. Give a person even a modicum of authority, and, if they're small in character, they will immediately use it to suppress those they deem a threat to their power.

I just returned from my annual visit to a Pennsylvania State Correctional Institute where I witnessed a correctional officer who, with his modicum of authority, delighted in humiliating the inmates and making their lives miserable. I've witnessed the same thing in TSA lines at airports, where small people have big authority. Often the only way they know to exert their authority is to rudely threaten and intimidate people.

As a society, we'd better take a good look at a person before we give him a badge and gun.

The culprit behind all this malicious invention is none other than Satan himself. After being dethroned from his heavenly position and defrocked of his cherubic authority, he found a most useful tool to control the world—despotic authority.

Satan tempted Jesus with the enticement of authority in Luke 4. "And the devil took him up and showed him all the kingdoms of the world in a moment of time, and said to him, 'To you I will give all this authority and their glory, for it has been delivered to me, and I give it to whom I will. If you, then, will worship me, it will all be yours'" (Luke 4:5-7).

I think that's the mantra of all evil leaders: "If you, then, will worship me, it will all be yours." Don't count on them actually giving the power to you, however. The purpose of the ploy is to increase their power *over* you. Notice that the promise of Communism to give all the workers of the world equality soon turned into the most despotic dictatorships the world has ever known.

Do you think Jesus actually believed that Satan would do what he said? Evil people don't delegate authority to anyone except those who have the same capacity to abuse and control people with it.

I've seen a host of leaders who exert authority in a demeaning, debilitating, and suppressing way and few who use it to build people up. Did you know that Satan loves to manipulate and deceive all of mankind into hating authority? As malevolent or insecure leaders exert their authority, those they rule start to hate authority. A vicious cycle begins to spin. Application of despotic authority is resented and resisted. As more of this negative authority is exerted by the leader, the people respond with higher and higher levels of animosity and resentment.

Twice in 2 Corinthians, Paul stated that authority was given to him for one reason only, and that was to build people up. "For even if I boast a little too much of our authority, which the Lord gave for building you up and not for destroying you, I will not be ashamed" (2 Corinthians 10:8).

He again says in 2 Corinthians 13:10: "For this reason I write these things while I am away from you, that when I come I may not have to be severe in my use of the authority that the Lord has given me for building up and not for tearing down."

All godly authority is given for the purpose of building people up! The use of authority should be beneficial and life-giving to the person you are mentoring. In the microcosm of teaching or discipling one person, you are using authority in the same way you would in the macrocosm of governing a group of people, a region, or a country.

When godly authority is exercised over the land, dry ditches fill with sparkling water and the people are suffused with new life, hope, and vibrancy. Authority must be used to construct and build, not to tear down and demolish. As soon as authority becomes oppressive and dictatorial, it becomes evil. And, importantly, when authority is not used to build people up, it ceases to be godly.

I've had one rule of thumb throughout my ministry: if a person wants authority, don't give it to them.

After I left the pastoral ministry in 2002 and Devi and I began Kingdom Global Ministries, I deliberately wrote the Constitution so it wouldn't include any form of authoritarian leadership. Why? Because I've done it wrong in the past and it never produces healthy people. If you like to be controlled and lorded over, you won't want to be part of our ministry.

Authority Is Necessary

If authority can be so deadly, why do we need it? Because without true, godly authority, you can't accomplish anything substantial and great. *But it must be the type of authority that releases people rather than controls them.*

- Godly authority releases people to fulfill their destiny. Abuse of power destroys initiative.
- Godly authority promotes people. Abuse of power demotes them.
- Godly authority is not oppressive, but liberating. Abuse of power subjugates people and brings them into bondage.
- Godly authority brings prosperity. Abuse of power brings poverty.
- Godly authority encourages people to be themselves. Abuse of power removes their identity and forces them to comply with external regulations.
- Godly authority produces peace. Abuse of power produces fear.
- Godly authority promotes righteousness. Abuse of power promotes sin and degradation.
- Godly authority solidifies a group. Abuse of power destroys it.
- Godly authority allows people the liberty to fail. Abuse of power punishes them if they do.

Godly authority allows people the liberty to fail.

- Godly authority encourages openness. Abusive authority promotes secrecy.

Unspeakable Abuse of Authority

During the Iraq War that began in March 2003, the United States Army and the Central Intelligence Agency committed a series of human rights violations against detainees in the Abu Ghraib prison, thirty miles west of Baghdad. These violations included physical and sexual abuse, torture, rape, sodomy, and murder. Pictures of what the army personnel did to the inmates became public and eventually led to the detention of seventeen soldiers and officers and the conviction of eleven.

It is sickening to see pictures of how those in responsibility mistreated the prisoners, humiliating, torturing, sodomizing, stripping naked, making men perform sex acts in front of them, and even gloating over the death of a prisoner. It's actually more disgusting than what I've described. This is what humans are capable of doing to other humans when given unlimited authority.

Prior to Abu Ghraib being used as a prison for men arrested during the US military occupation of Iraq, it was used as a prison for 50,000 inmates during the dictatorial reign of

Saddam Hussein. I'm sure the atrocities committed during the Hussein regime would make the US violations look tame, but I'm not comparing. In both cases, in the same location, people with a degree of power and authority used it to destroy, not build up, the detainees.

Authority can be either destructive or constructive in the hands of the leader. When used for evil, it leads to unimaginable horrors.

Jesus the Delegator

In the Upper Room on resurrection evening, Jesus greeted the disciples with the words, "As the Father has sent me, even so I am sending you" (John 20:21). There cannot be a clearer demonstration in scripture of the correct use of authority. Someone with authority, in this case the Father, delegated it to Jesus, and Jesus delegated it to the disciples. There is a certain spiritual genealogy or succession in the granting of this true authority. Godly leaders pass it down to the next generation of spiritually-fit leaders as Jesus did with His disciples.

The essential and unconditional relationship Jesus held with His disciples allowed them to grow into men who could receive His authority. Jesus allowed these men to walk with Him for a relatively short period of three and a half years. They became men who could receive and exercise His authority. Jesus chiseled and shaped these men into characters who could compassionately carry the weight of authority He gave them. And, germane to the topic of this book, He left us the techniques and methods of His discipleship and teaching.

That's why Peter and John felt comfortable telling the lame man at the Gate Beautiful that they didn't have silver or gold, but they had authority—the name of Jesus. Jesus gave them authority to use His name, so they chose to try it out. In a similar measure, God gives leaders freedom to give godly authority away.

The final words of Jesus before ascending to heaven were: "All authority in heaven and on earth has been given to me" (Matthew 28:18-19). After speaking those words, Jesus gave the disciples His full authority, beginning with the words, "Go therefore and make disciples . . ."

Had Jesus not delegated His authority to His disciples, the entire purpose of His life on earth would have failed and His ongoing ministry truncated. If a leader does not delegate his authority to others, then his works stop when he dies, or in many cases while he's still alive. It was necessary that the Author of our Salvation deputize His disciples to carry on His work. The redemptive purpose of the cross would have stopped with His ascension if Jesus hadn't prepared His successors to receive and release His authority.

How is the Gospel the "Good News" if no one has been given the authority to share it? What kind of leader would Jesus be if no one followed Him, or no future leaders could receive and run with the torch? If Jesus alone could heal the sick, cast out demons, or raise the dead, how could the world be reached after His departure? That's the reason He designated first the twelve, then the seventy, and finally the 120 to carry on His work (see Matthew 10; Luke 10; Acts 1:8, 15).

Jesus, a Good Head

Jesus was a good "Head." Good "heads" delegate their authority to the body, and never do all the work themselves. As good as a leader might be in organizing, strategizing, and administrating, there is not one thing he can do without the hands, legs, feet, and internal organs to carry out the plan, and unless the members of the body have been delegated to do the work of the ministry, they are frustrated at best and paralyzed at worst.

Many leaders micromanage because they're afraid of losing their authority, power, and recognition. I've heard numerous pastors say the reason they don't want to have small groups is because someone could gain too much authority. I don't think Jesus would have feared that. A pastor who tightly clings to his own authority might be considered a spiritually dangerous man.

Good leaders always delegate; they always release authority to their disciples. Yet we have many leaders who never delegate their authority to others. They are the beginning and the end of their own ministry. They are self-appointed "Alpha and Omega" men and women; leaders who have no lineage, no disciples, no "sent" ones to carry on their work. They are "heads" without "bodies." When their leadership is over, it's *really* over. The only thing left after their departure is a massive leadership vacuum, which Satan is all too eager to fill.

It's a Scary Thing

Delegation is a scary thing. How do you know your disciples will do it like you did? You don't. How do you know you can trust those whom you have trained? You don't. How do you know that your authority won't be turned against you when you leave? You don't. How do you know your ministry will increase rather than decrease after your departure? You don't. How do you know your disciples will remain loyal? You have no idea. You have to trust Jesus, the Head of the Church, for everything, and entrust authority into the hands of others. You must delegate authority, or you remain a one-man show, with no possibility of fulfilling the Great Commission. So, you either delegate or you will have a stagnant ministry, and when you die, everything you've done will also die.

Devi and I recently spoke at two different churches in the same city in Brazil, on the same weekend. One was healthy, the other extremely weak and close to dying. The healthy church had raised up dozens of great leaders, including the pastor's wife, daughter, son, son-in-law, and staff pastors; even their youngest son was already preaching on the streets of the city. If, God forbid, something would happen to the pastor, there was a long line of equally qualified and gifted leaders who could step up to his position.

The other church had recently lost its dynamic, unilateral, evangelistic, inspirational leader. He had built a large following, a large, cavernous building, and a lot of beautiful facilities. Unfortunately, he never delegated or released his authority to others. No one knew what he did. No one was trained as a successor. No one was allowed to know information that only he knew. He was an Abraham without an Isaac. There was no posterity to carry on his legacy except his aged wife, who struggled to maintain the momentum. It wasn't working. The massive building was empty. I had the feeling that the few dozen people who attended came to hear us, and after we were gone, so were they. That is what happens when people fail to delegate.

It Relates to Your Family Too

The husband, as the head of the wife, has the same responsibilities as any other leader. To have a healthy family and marriage, he must delegate; he must hand some of his authority over to his spouse and family. By doing this, he will see his wife flourish as she holds what you entrusted to her. His children will walk uprightly, encouraged by the faith and trust given them.

The greatest joy in life is seeing your wife and children fully released to become all they are in Christ. But they cannot be released unless you release your authority to them. Healthy fathers are not afraid to release their authority to their family. *For authority to be healthy it must be shared, and it should start with the family.*

Have you seen a man sitting in the stands at a baseball game and watching his son play? Have you seen the son look to his father before going up to bat? The dad delights in his son's play and the son steps into the batter's box warmed and animated by his father's faith and encouragement. The father shows us how a leader should feel—a heart delighted by his disciples as he releases them into their ministry and vision.

Delegating and transferring your authority is not just a matter of leadership genealogy and continuity. If you don't delegate, you will never have the wondrous reward of seeing your followers fully released into their calling and bringing their "A" game. Nothing gratifies me more than hearing my spiritual sons say, "My dad is the one who trained and released me." Remember, the only way not to be a big head with a little body is to delegate, thus bringing glory to God and honor to your posterity. Babies, with their disproportionately large heads, are so cute. However, if the head continued to grow as fast as the body grew, it would soon become a monstrosity. The head remains essentially the same size, yet the body continues to grow to conform to the size of the head. Leaders, concentrate on growing your body, your people, your congregation, your family.

Transferring or delegating authority to others doesn't mean the leader doesn't continue to maintain and exercise authority. Without authority, nothing gets accomplished. But we must find ways to change our leadership style so that it continues to release rather than suppress people. I don't want the people I lead to cower under my authority; I want them to be empowered and emboldened. I want them to accomplish their vision.

Years ago, I became pastor of a congregation in Amarillo, Texas. I had been there only one year when the Lord spoke to me what I was to do. His directive was actually very blunt. Sitting in my car, waiting for a friend to arrive for a lunch appointment, I heard the Lord clearly say, "You're not the pastor."

I couldn't believe what I was hearing.

"I'm not the pastor? If I'm not the pastor, who is?"

"Jimmy Evans," was the Lord's reply.

Jimmy was a faithful member of our church. He spent his days working in his father's appliance business. He was a leader in one of the home groups and was always adding more chairs. He was a people magnet. His teaching gifts were obvious. Wisdom poured out of him like a river.

I brought Jimmy into my office and told him what I had heard the Lord speak to me, not knowing that less than a year and a half later, I would resign and turn the leadership of the church over to him.

I knew Jimmy and his wife Karen were gifted, but I had no idea how gifted they really were. Through Jimmy and Tom Lane, his executive assistant, the church grew from a few hundred people to thousands, seemingly overnight. At the same time, Jimmy's teaching on marriage and family began reaching hundreds of thousands of people. Today, through television and conferences, they touch *millions* of marriages, with a weekly television audience of over 100 million people. Trinity Fellowship of Churches, under Jimmy's leadership, brought many dozens of churches into their organization. It's hard to convey the power of delegation to release individual ministries and expand the Body of Christ globally.

I can take no credit for what God has done through this amazing, anointed couple. As far as I can tell, the only thing I did was delegate authority to Jimmy and give him the opportunity to lead. The results were pure Jimmy and the Holy Spirit in him.

But that's not the end. Jimmy Evans and Tom Lane apostolically sent Pastor Robert Morris to begin a ministry in the greater Dallas/Fort Worth, Texas area. In 2000, Pastor Morris established Gateway Church in Southlake, Texas, which now

How sweet and savory is the fruit of a godly transfer of authority!

ministers weekly to over 30,000 people. Pastor Morris has become one of the nation's most influential leaders.

That's called delegation. How sweet and savory is the fruit of a godly transfer of authority!

But that's also not the end of the story. Gateway Church, through Robert Morris's training and releasing leadership, continues to spark ministries throughout the nation and world. Again, that's delegation! Leaders who are confident in their own gifts don't find it necessary to suppress the gifts of others. Authority, like everything else God has given to us, was meant to be given away.

Never fear the result of delegation. Never fear the product of releasing authority to others. You can leave it all up to God. *None of us possess those we lead.* We can only lead them by example. You have a lot to gain and little to lose if you choose to lead God's way, by delegating your authority to capable men and women with passion and vision.

When we use authority to suppress people, we line up behind a long line of evil dictators. When we use authority to release people in their callings, we line up directly behind Jesus Christ.

I pray you will find ways to delegate and release your authority to others. That's the only way to guarantee your authority will remain pure and reach future generations. You will watch with delight the fruit of those you have taught and released. You will echo the Father, who opened the heavens after Jesus was baptized, proudly saying these are your sons and you are well pleased with them. Delegate and release others and you will decide your own legacy, and you will be that rare leader who *leads differently*.

CHAPTER 7

Lead
with unconditional love

*I have found the paradox that
if I love until it hurts, then there
is no hurt, but only more love.*

Mother Teresa

*"A new commandment I give to you, that you love one
another: just as I have loved you, you also are to love
one another."*

John 13:34

Years ago, when trains were a more common mode of transportation, a businessman was rushing to catch a train bound for New York City. In his hurry, he slammed directly into the display rack of a boy selling wares. He hit the rack so hard that all the merchandise was scattered across the platform. The disconcerted boy sadly surveyed the mess. In the dank-smelling air, the man saw his train about to pull out of the station. He had to make a quick decision.

He sighed and bent down to comfort the boy and help pick up the merchandise, knowing full well he would miss his appointment.

The boy looked up at the businessman and said, "Mister, are you Jesus?"

What was it that reminded the boy of Jesus? Was it the man's tailored business suit, his perfectly-groomed appearance, or the briefcase he carried? No, it was the love of the strange man who elevated the boy's welfare above his professional demands.

Love always says, "You're more important."

A Relentless Love

What the man did was a miniscule sample of what Jesus did daily. He put other people's interests ahead of His own. To Him, sinners were more important than saints; affirmation more important than criticism; healing more important than condemnation. The common man was more important to Jesus than religious leaders. He fondly embraced the disadvantaged above those with influence and renown.

He touched disfigured lepers when doing so would make Him unclean and temporarily disqualify Him from entering the temple precincts. He allowed Himself to be touched by a woman with an unceasing flow of blood, marking Himself unclean under Jewish law—both contaminated and untouchable. When she began to shrink back from Him, He looked for her in the crowd, calling her His "Daughter."

Rather than overlooking people who the culture rejected, Jesus *pursued* them, inviting them to look into His face and receive a love that elevates.

Eating with sinners and tax collectors was foul and despicable to the religious zealots, but no problem for Jesus. Maybe His biggest gaffe, or so the zealots thought, was a public conversation with a Samaritan woman, the lowest of the low, disgraced because of her heritage. Per Jewish law, talking with her also made Jesus unclean and barred Him from the exclusive company of the literati of His day.

Apparently, when love was needed, Jesus was oblivious to what was socially acceptable.

Love Always Won

Had the Jewish bigots heard the conversation between Jesus and the Samaritan woman, they would have been mortified. There at Jacob's ancient well, Jesus told this despised woman with multiple lovers His most guarded secrets. Before most others knew, it was revealed to the Samaritan woman that Jesus was the long-awaited Jewish Messiah. Like an outpouring of living water directly from the well, Jesus poured His love over her. Whereas He could have condemned her, instead He gave her His most precious and guarded truth.

Every page of the Gospel's revelation of Jesus Christ is printed in ink squeezed from His love. Page after page writes the story of His ardent and persistent love for the disciples, His vast and panoramic love for the multitudes, and His authentic and unequivocal love for the downtrodden.

Rather than avoid proximity to the demon-possessed and the adulterers, Jesus showed a relentless love that delivered and healed. What could be more passionate than His love for the children, expressed in Matthew chapters 18, 19, and 21, and His ultimate love for the Father, expressed 120 times in the Gospel of John? I am convinced that no one can love others in depth until they love the Father expansively. The Father is the Fountainhead of all love, the source from which all rivers of love flow.

The Beginning of Love

Evidently Jesus' love relationship with the Father began before the creation of the world and extended from eternity to eternity (John 17:1, 2, 5, 24, 26; Revelation 13:8). Of course, nothing expresses the love of Jesus for the Father greater than the crucifixion. If laying down one's life for a friend is the greatest expression of earthly love (John 15:13), then the love that led Jesus to the cross defies description. All measurement is stripped away as one attempts to describe the depth, width, height, and breadth of Jesus' love for the Father expressed on the cross.

The prelude to this agony came in the Garden of Gethsemane, when great drops of blood and sweat were forced through Jesus' capillaries and fell to the ground: "Father, if you are willing, remove this cup from me. Nevertheless, not my will, but yours, be done" (Luke 22:42). Have you ever witnessed such love? Have you ever engaged such a Savior? Sadness must have enveloped His heart and tears clouded His eyes as He moved away from the place of travail and found the disciples sleeping. The flesh has limits, but love has none.

After three and a half years of walking among mankind, Jesus finally carried His cross up the lonely hill called Golgotha for the sins of the world. Never had the universe seen an act of love of such magnitude. We believers must return over and over to this sacrifice and be astounded anew. As He offered the gift of life, Jesus had no hidden agenda. He showed love as He took the lashes, wore the crown of thorns, and surrendered His hands and feet to the brutal spikes. The love of Christ was persistent and unrelenting, forming His final words of forgiveness as He died in agony. On the cross, we even hear His love in the caring commendation of His mother to His disciple John.

Love's Long Embrace

If the greatest demonstration of love, according to Jesus, was for a man to lay down his life for his friends (John 15:13), Jesus went well beyond that. He laid down His life for the vilest of sinners, the down-and-out, the self-righteous bigots—and who would die for them? If you want to know how low love's embrace reached, Jesus went all the way to Hades and destroyed the power of death (Revelation 1:18; Hebrews 2:14).

On the opposite extreme, when He ascended from the grave, He took with Him to Paradise all the righteous of the Old Testament, including the man crucified with Him (Luke 23:43; Ephesians 4:8). That's love's long embrace.

Romans 8:35, 37-38 says it all: "Who shall separate us from the love of Christ? Shall tribulation, or distress, or persecution, or famine, or nakedness, or danger, or sword? No, in all these things we are more than conquerors through him who loved us. For I am sure that neither death nor life, nor angels nor rulers, nor things present nor things to come, nor powers, nor height nor depth, nor anything else in all creation, will be able to separate us from the love of God in Christ Jesus our Lord."

In Psalm 103:12, the psalmist describes the Messiah's love as broad and wide as the East is from the West. (Thank God there are no East or West poles where my sins can be found, shamefully waiting for me.) This love is deeper than the lowest hell and higher than the highest heaven.

The Ink of Love

In the early 20th century, a Christian workingman and hymnist named Frederick Lehman wrote a hymn about the love of God. The chorus of the great hymn reads:

O love of God, how rich and pure!
How measureless and strong!
It shall forevermore endure
The saints' and angels' song.

The hymn originally contained only two stanzas. However, when thinking of a third stanza, Lehman remembered that a friend had handed him a grimy piece of paper with a handwritten verse that had been penciled decades earlier on the wall of a mental institution. An unknown inmate had written this verse, most likely recalled from the original words penned over a thousand years ago by the Jewish Rabbi, Meir Ben Issac Nehoria, from Worms, Germany.

How this verse made its way from the famed rabbi, down to the anonymous inmate in a mental institution, to the scrawled note handed to Frederick Lehman, we'll never know. But I do know that love has the power to transcend generations and continents, reaching its long embrace to this book. I have never found a better description of the vastness of the love of God.

> *Could we with ink the ocean fill / And were the skies of parchment made,*
> *Were every stalk on earth a quill / And every man a scribe by trade,*
> *To write the love of God above / Would drain the ocean dry.*
> *Nor could the scroll contain the whole / Though stretched from sky to sky.*

Just try to absorb the truth of these words.

Probably, because I've crossed it so many times in my fifteen-hour flights to Australia, my mind instantly recalls the Pacific Ocean. This magnificent body of water measures 63.8 million square miles. Its widest point stretches 12,300 miles, greeting Indonesia and Colombia. The deepest part of the Pacific is the Mariana Trench, 36,070 feet deep. Our

> # Love reshapes itself
> # in order to fill any
> # vacuum.

hymnist, rabbi, and inmate ask us to imagine what it would be like to try to fathom the fathomless love of God.

If we could fill the Pacific with ink, that would amount to approximately 710,000,000 cubic kilometers of black pigmented liquid. That's a lot of ink. Consider now that all the earth's stalks of grain are actually pens, quills, or other writing instruments, and every person living on earth is a scribe.

We are now ready to write the message of God's love. But what could possibly suffice for the writing material of such a herculean task? Our poets beg we consider looking up to the skies for parchment. Rather than seeing the massive expanse of sky as patches of cumulus, stratus, and cirrus clouds, we imagine it as one endless stretch of parchment.

Seven billion inhabitants of earth pick up their quills and write the love of God on the papery expanse.

But a conundrum ensues. If we were to write God's love on the heavenly expanse, it would drain the oceans dry, and the skies could not contain the length of the scroll.

Leaders and Love

Love is the greatest force in the world. No leader can effectively lead without it. Love is the most palpable intangible. Though you can't touch it, you can feel it instantly. You can sense when it is around you. You can bask in it and enjoy its warmth. You can feel its security. You welcome its acceptance. Lack of love stings just as quickly. If just a drop of God's love were to touch our lips, it would cleanse us from criticism, divisiveness, hatred, gossip, contempt, judgmentalism, bias, lying, inequity, anger, and all forms of violence and abuse.

The greatest need in the world is not education, jobs, military dominance, climate stability, good governance, gender equality, refugee intervention, or even peace. The greatest need in the world is love. *Love reshapes itself in order to fill any vacuum. Even fear evaporates when you are filled with love.* If you have enough love, you have no need.

Jesus Said It This Way

"You shall love the Lord your God with all your heart and with all your soul and with all your mind. This is the great and first commandment. And a second is like it: You shall love your neighbor as yourself" (Matthew 22:37-39).

How can you love anyone else if you cannot love yourself? It all begins with your love for God. Without that unabashed, unrestricted, reckless love for God, you will never love yourself or others. Loving others helps us love ourselves. I don't love myself first; I love God first and love others second as God commands, and in return, self-love is the natural result.

Self-loathing seems to be ubiquitous. For those from religious backgrounds, it might even seem spiritual. In my many years of ministry I've found far more people who felt deep dissatisfaction with themselves than healthy self-worth. If

God made you in His image, it is important to value yourself rather than despise who you are. If you are the exact image and likeness of God (Genesis 1:26-27), then I find no reason why anyone would not embrace who God made them to be.

The Hebrew word for "good" is *tov*. When God created all the different elements of creation, He called them *tov*. But when He created man, God said he was *tov, tov*, "good, good." I hope you realize how really *tov, tov* you are. A good, good God has created a good, good you.

To take it a step further, I cannot think of one person I've ever met who spoke value into others, especially those closest to them, when they saw no value in themselves. Without a sense of love for yourself, how can you dispense love to others? Of course, this is all predicated on loving God with all your heart, mind, and soul first.

I grew up with very low self-esteem, which expressed itself in aloofness, timidity, and total self-absorption. Suffering from low self-esteem causes a person to become more absorbed with self than those with a healthy self-image. I also had a tendency toward moodiness, moroseness, and unhealthy introspection, all of which alienated me from the very people I wanted to love.

Self-loathing Isn't Spiritual

After enduring more than four years of depression, I can tell you beyond a shadow of a doubt that self-absorption is deadly. It's a wonder anyone stuck with me. The only topic of discussion, at least in my own head, was, "How do *I* feel?" It was all about me. "Me" was my only focus. Only when I began to see value in myself was I able to break the unbearable yoke of depression.

Seeing value in yourself is neither narcissistic, arrogant, nor presumptuous. It is viewing yourself as God sees you: a person of value. Ironically, to heap false humility, deprecation, and self-flagellation upon yourself never produces love for others, but rather self-righteousness, the opposite of love. This is pseudo-humility, the antithesis of brokenness.

If only we could have experienced unqualified love from our parents, maybe we would have had a glimpse of how much God the Father loves us. But for most of us, that was not an option. The love of God, expressed in Jesus Christ, is the foundation for all true love relationships. We cannot even truly love ourselves, our spouse, or anyone else until we sense how great the Father's love is for us. If we can get that down, everything else will fall into place.

When you begin to view yourself as God sees you, you will discover a whole new world of love for others. When I traded my low self-esteem for a sense of value in Jesus, love began to flow like a river. Now I love everyone. I love strangers; I love family; I love enemies; I love people I see on television; I love people I meet at the airport. Hardly a day goes by that I don't pray for total strangers I see or meet on the streets. I cannot explain to you the depth of love I have for people. It began when I started to view myself as God sees me: imperfect, but valuable and loved.

Seeing value in yourself is not self-centered, but God-centered. If you're not agreeing with God's opinion of you, there's only one other option: to agree with the Accuser of the Brethren, Satan himself. Since the devil is a liar and the father of lies, I would suggest that you don't stay attached to him or his opinion of you.

Jack Deere, one of my favorite authors, has recently released a book titled *Even in Our Darkness*. In the book, Deere tells the story of how his favorite seminary professor, Dr. Waltke, gave him an assignment to find the meaning of the preposition *to* in the first line of Psalm 139:17-18:

> *How precious* to *me are your thoughts, O God!*
> *How vast is the sum of them!*
> *If I would count them,*
> *they are more than the sand.*

Quoting Jack:

> In English, the word *to* can be used in at least twenty ways, and these can be summarized in a single paragraph. But the standard Hebrew lexicon devoted eight-and-a-half large, double-columned, fine-print pages to the preposition *to*. There are hundreds of ways to use it.
>
> After I spent hours reading through all the relevant examples in the lexicon, I was sure that the traditional translation *"to me"* in verse 17 had to be wrong.
>
> The verse should be translated:
>
> *How precious are your thoughts* about me, *God!*
>
> *How vast is the sum of them!*
>
> *Were I to count them,*

They would outnumber the grains of sand.

A preposition changed the entire meaning of these two verses. God's thoughts about me outnumbered the grains of the earth's sand—even when it was far from my mind. Studying the various uses of *to* had unlocked another realm of profundity about God's boundless love for me.[1]

This statement by Jack Deere stopped me dead in my tracks. God's love for me is greater than the grains of the earth's sand. Unfathomable. Unimaginable. Incomprehensible. Uncountable. How does my love for others compare with that of my Father?

Love Is Who God Is

Love, in its many forms, is often inexplicable. At times it's detectable by the human senses. You can feel when it's there and you know when it's not. People can discern it radiating from you even at a distance. Children can sense it immediately. Hardened criminals break into tears at merely the hint that someone loves them. Even animals know if you love them.

Love is not only a facet of God's nature; it is the sum total of who He is. 1 John 4:16 puts it succinctly: "God is love." Like turning a diamond with many facets, each one reveals another aspect of God's love. God is so loving that He loves even those who don't love Him, including those who never will. Don't forget, He is the source of love, the disseminator of love, and in

---

1. Jack Deere, *Even in Our Darkness: A Story of Beauty in a Broken Life* (Grand Rapids: Zondervan, 2018), 118.

Jesus, the embodiment of love. God's will is that all mankind choose to be vessels of love, reflections of His image.

Because love is reflective, it is found everywhere. Beaming from the very heart of God, there is no place so remote that someone is not at this very moment revealing the heart of God through the expression of love. Songs are being sung; babies are being cradled; hardened soldiers are mourning the death of a comrade or innocent victim; dads are embracing prodigal sons; grievances are being mended; relationships are being restored; lyricists are writing songs; food and clothing is being distributed; first responders are putting their lives at risk to save people; romance is in full bloom; tears, smiles, hugs, giving, and joy all reveal the love of God.

Most of us cannot comprehend unqualified love. Why? Because we've never experienced it! Most people receive skimpy expressions of love if they win the game, achieve good grades, look beautiful, do a job well, or excel in something. If love has to be earned, then it isn't God's love at all. God's love is a gift. A prize of love gained by doing good things or excelling at something is counterfeit love. It is not the love of God. It is only and nothing more than a reward for good works.

An even larger group of people don't even get the opportunity to earn qualified love, because they aren't loved from the beginning. Insecure, absentee, or dysfunctional parents made sure that their children didn't receive even a modicum of love, not even love that had been earned. Left out from the beginning, they didn't even enjoy the "reward" of qualified love.

One teenage girl in Brazil told us of the day when her mother, sitting across the table from her, said, "You're so ugly I don't ever want to see your face again." The teenage girl left home, never to return. I can't imagine any parent making such cruel comments to their children. Neither can I grasp the beauty of God's love as it was expressed through pastors in her city who brought her into the church, introduced her to Jesus, hired her, and eventually made her their lead worship leader. *Hatred and bigotry casts people out, but love draws them in.*

The Greeks and Love

There are three main Greek words for love—*eros, phileo,* and *agape.* Though *phileo,* brotherly love, is used on occasion to describe God's love, *agape* is the main word in the New Testament used to define the unconditional love God has for us and that we are to have for each other. *Eros* expresses sexual and sensual love and is not mentioned in the Bible. *Phileo* describes love that collegial friends have for each other—a friendship type of non-sexual, platonic love.

When Jesus questioned Peter's love for Him following the resurrection, Peter was unable to respond to *agape* love. Twice Jesus asked Peter, "Simon, son of John, do you love [*agape*] me?" Peter's response to both questions found him changing the word from *agape* to *phileo.* "Yes, Lord; you know that I love [*phileo*] you." Roughly translated, that means, "Yes, Lord, I'm fond of you."

Jesus then changed Greek words: Peter, do you *phileo* love me? Peter could then answer in the affirmative. "Yes, Lord, I love you as a friend." John 21:15-19

I'm sure Peter was being totally honest. Most likely his own sense of shame and embarrassment at denouncing Jesus in the courtyard wouldn't allow him to rise to that level of *agape,* God's love. Obviously, things changed. It was Peter, the one

Agape love doesn't burn bridges.

who battled feelings of shame, guilt, and unworthiness, who penned the words: "Above all, keep loving [*agape*] one another earnestly, since love [*agape*] covers a multitude of sins" (1 Peter 4:8). Who would know better than Peter what type of love it was that could cover a multitude of sins?

If God's love can restore Peter, it can restore anyone.

In addition to decades of loyal service to Jesus, tradition holds that in AD 64, Peter requested of his executioners that he be crucified upside down, because he was unworthy to be crucified in the same manner as Jesus. Love, said Jesus, is willing to lay down its life for a friend (John 15:13). When love is willing to die for a friend, it then becomes *agape* love.

Unqualified Love

Agape delineates and identifies God's unqualified love. It is an unmerited gift sent specifically to you. You can't earn it and you can't lose it. It's a gift to you wrapped in the luminous fullness of God's eternal commitment. You weren't given this gift because of something you did; it's God's eternal gift to you, never to be rescinded. But, like a giftbox, you must receive it and open it to experience its impact in your life. God's love for you is not finicky or capricious, nor will His love be changed because of circumstances.

Agape love makes no demands on the person being loved. It simply says, "You don't have to do anything for me to love you." There are no ulterior motives.

Agape love doesn't burn bridges. Neither will God cut people off when they displease or fail Him. This is how you should express your love as a mentor, teacher, and disciple-maker. Your love should be consistent, unmovable, and without equivocation. Your intent should be that nothing can remove your forever love from someone.

Some people have burned so many bridges that little remains on which to build a loving future. These folks are so easily offended, they carry their matches and lighter fluid with them wherever they go. Any potential slight or offense results in a bonfire, and the relationship dissolves into ashes. Dealing with relationships with matches is easy and conclusive, but an opportunity for a lifetime of love goes up in smoke.

My mother-in-law is the ultimate example of unqualified love. To her great-grandson who had stolen money, credit cards, and even her truck, she replied, "There are two things you can never make me do. You can never make me angry, and you can never make me stop loving you." That's what unqualified love looks like.

The Gospels show us that God expects us to act just like His Son as He lived His life on earth. If who I am and what I do displays love, only then do I look like Jesus. My leadership is only a reflection of Jesus' leadership when I choose to impersonate or replicate His life.

Agape Love

Here are five characteristics of God's love:

First, God's agape love is unqualified. Love that is conditional or provisional is not the love of God. There are no in-betweens here. The type of love that says "If you do this then I'll love you" is foreign to the Gospels. "If you come to my church then I'll love you." "If you pass this exam then I'll love you." "If you do it my way then I'll love you." "If you win the game then I'll love you." These are conditional statements of love. Conditional love is not the *agape* love flowing from the heart of God. *True love, God's love, gives but expects nothing in return.* There can be no "if" qualifiers in love. *If love is qualified, then it is disqualified.*

Second, agape love is totally selfless. It always says, "You're first." "You're more important." "I prefer you." No wonder sinners loved Jesus. Unlike the Pharisees, He didn't ask them to become ritually good and clean before He loved them. He loved them just as they were. They followed Him for days just to touch the hem of His garment. Sinners poured perfume on His feet because they felt loved and accepted; they climbed trees just to see Him; they invited Him to their homes so they could dine with Him. His love was so effusive and powerful it poured out like a river and they just wanted to touch Him.

Third, love refuses to hold grudges. It freely offers forgiveness. It does not keep a record of wrongs. The love expressed in Jesus' final words, "Father, forgive them, for they know not what they do" (Luke 23:34), should be our beginning words. No greater love can a person show than to give his life for a friend. But dying for sinners? "But God demonstrates his own love for us in this: While we were still sinners, Christ died for us" (Romans 5:8 NIV). In this verse is a principle, hidden yet powerful in its truth and redemptive potential: it is nearly as difficult to forgive someone as it is to die for them. Forgiveness is essential as you apply *agape* love.

Fourth, love is a choice. If you think love is an emotion or feeling that comes and goes, you will never understand God's love! Your own life will be unstable! I *choose* to love people. I love people so deeply it hurts at times. *Agape* love is an action, not a feeling. I'm pre-set from God's creative factory to love people. It's in my nature because it is in my Heavenly Father's nature. Anything other than that doesn't come from God the Father.

Fifth, love has no impact unless it is believed. God's love for you is greater than anything you can comprehend, but you can't receive it until you believe it. Neither can your spouse, family, or friends receive your love until they truly believe you love them. That insight, by the way, came from my wife, and I *believe* she loves me, therefore I receive it.

You Are God's Love Agent

How does God express love? Of course, He can always send angels, or put us in circumstances or places where love is demonstrated. But that's generally not His modus operandi. *The majority of time, God sends a person who will convey His love; someone who extends such unqualified, unmerited love that they look just like God. And you could be just that person.*

If you want an example of God's love as it operates through a person, read the book *The Hiding Place*, by Corrie ten Boom.

When you make the choice to love someone, God moves through you in all His fullness. In Corrie's case, God compelled her to love the Nazi concentration camp guard who killed her sister. She said that when she chose to forgive her sister's murderer, it was like electricity passing through her body. Through forgiveness, she was baptized in love. Corrie then became an agent of God's love throughout the world. Everywhere she went, people were transformed by the effusive river of love that poured out of her.

On the day I sat in front of Corrie and heard her speak in Munich, Germany in 1972, I felt literally baptized in love. As she spoke, it was like a river of love splashed out on me, inundating me with the incomprehensible depth of God's love. I will never forget that moment. On that day, I decided that I too would become an agent of God's love. It's my goal that everywhere I go, everyone I meet will experience the ocean of God's love, an ocean to swim in.

It might be too early to order the epitaph I want on my tombstone, but just for the record, I want it to read, "He loved God and he loved people." That says it all.

Love Does

It's easy to love people who love you, but infinitely more difficult to love those who don't reciprocate, or even stand maliciously against you. Jesus continued to love the disciples after every single one walked out on Him in His darkest moment in the garden. He loved Peter who denied Him three times during His courtyard interrogation.

Love can be expressed through giving, serving, physical expressions, and most of all, dying for the one you love. In our daily lives, a powerful expression of love is to speak words of affirmation. I've heard so many men say they love their wives, but their words belie that fact. I've heard women continually berate their husbands and then insist that they love them. It doesn't sound like it. How can you love someone and speak to them or about them with rancor and impatience?

Love is patient, kind, does not envy, does not boast, is not arrogant, is not rude, is not easily offended, is not easily angered, doesn't remember all the wrongs a person has done, doesn't rejoice in an evil report but rejoices in the truth. And Paul is right—it is the only thing that endures into eternity (1 Corinthians 13).

If we do not love people with *agape* love, we do not accurately portray the heart of the Father, who is defined by one word: "God is *love*" (1 John 4:16). If people don't feel affirmed and loved by us, then our message is in vain. People will know that you truly love them when they look for an ulterior motive for your affection, but fail to find one.

Jesus made it clear that the defining mark of a disciple is not going to church or even saying you're a Christian, but love. "By this all people will know that you are my disciples, if you have love for one another" (John 13:35).

If you aspire to leadership, you must put yourself under a microscope. You must examine everything that motivates you to lead and disciple. If love provokes you and inspires you, and love is your underlying and prime motivator, you will be a great leader. Without love, your leadership will be as annoying as clanging cymbals.

Ultimate Love

God's greatest gift of love was His Son, Jesus, sent to die a horrible death so that we might experience expansive, eternal life. The world's most favorite and oft-quoted verse says it all: "For God so loved the world that he gave his one and only Son, that whoever believes in him shall not perish but have eternal life" (John 3:16 NIV). The crosses that dangle gracefully from the ends of chains, adorning so many necks; the crosses on a thousand church steeples stretching high over cityscapes; the headstones of untold millions of people; even the dark tattoos inked on human skin, cannot compare with the grotesque silhouette of a blood-stained tree upon which hung the limp victim of Roman "justice."

If you want to see what God's love looks like, expressed through His Son, look to Calvary, or Golgotha, the place of the skull. Through the mist of two thousand years of history, we see a man who loved until there was no more life left in Him. Through swollen eyes and parched lips, His final words were, "Father, forgive them, for they know not what they do" (Luke 23:34). Love never looked so pitiful yet so grand. Love never boasted a greater victory than the death of the sinless Son dying for sinful man. If you want to *lead differently*, learn how to lead by love.

CHAPTER 8

Lead
by telling stories

*If history were taught in the
form of stories, it would never
be forgotten.*

Rudyard Kipling

*"He told many stories in the form of parables, such as
this one: 'Listen! A farmer went out to
plant some seeds.'"*

Matthew 13:3 NLT

In only five minutes, we forget.

Most church attendees walk out of the service, shaking hands and being social. By the time they exit the front door of the church, they have already forgotten what the sermon was about. They remember they liked or disliked it, but they don't remember the substance of the text. Five minutes! That's as long as a song on the radio. What's this about?

Jesus spent 70% of His time, whether teaching the disciples or the multitudes, using a parabolic form of communication. Only 30% of the time did He use a lecture style of teaching. In other words, He drew mental pictures with parables so people could visualize His message.

Teachers who use only a lecture style, without drawing pictures with their words, are not only sure to be forgotten, but can also be counted on to put people to sleep in a relatively short time. A listener's eyes, imagination, and heart must be connected to his ears or he will likely forget what he hears. If you want people to remember your message, stoke their imagination by drawing mental photo images through illustrations, examples, personal experiences, testimonies, parables, and metaphors.

The Power of the Story

Jesus chose a parabolic style as the primary way of conveying kingdom principles. For example, there are eight parables in Matthew 13 alone. Jesus started most of His illustrations by saying, "The kingdom of heaven is like," then He drew a mental picture that could be imagined and remembered.

"The kingdom of heaven is like":

. . . *a man who sowed good seed in his field* :(verse 24). Can you visualize a farmer sowing seed?

. . . *a grain of mustard seed* (verse 31). Have you ever seen how small a mustard seed is? You'd better grab a magnifying glass or you'll miss it.

. . . *leaven that a woman took and hid in three measures of flour* (verse 33). Any baker can easily visualize the raising power of yeast.

. . . *a treasure hidden in a field* (verse 44). That would fuel any boy's imagination of pirates and hidden treasures.

. . . *a merchant in search of fine pearls* (verse 45). Before the age of cultured pearls, one single pearl could fetch a huge amount of money.

. . . *a net that was thrown into the sea* (verse 47). Fishermen would know exactly what Jesus was talking about.

. . . *a master of a house, who brings out of his treasure what is new and what is old* (verse 52). I love showing people my art treasures when they visit my home. Some pieces go back hundreds of years. Two pages from the First Edition of the King James Bible, printed in 1611, are always a draw for first-time visitors.

Jesus illustrated His messages by using nature to vivdly describe eternal truths.

Unforgettable

Jesus illustrated His messages by using nature to vividly describe eternal truths. He drew pictures with soil, storms, wheat, flowers, and the farming process of sowing and reaping so we could picture not just the concepts of the kingdom, but the actions of the kingdom.

In His concluding remarks to the Sermon on the Mount, Jesus gives us a poignant illustration:

> Everyone then who hears these words of mine and does them will be like a wise man who built his house on the rock. And the rain fell, and the floods came, and the winds blew and beat on that house, but it did not fall, because it had been founded on the rock. And everyone who hears these words of mine and does not do them will be like a foolish man who built his house on the sand. And the rain fell, and the floods came, and the winds blew and beat against that house, and it fell, and great was the fall of it. (Matthew 7:24-27)

As one who grew up in California, I vividly remember the pictures of homes sliding off the sides of a mountain and into the Pacific Ocean because they were not built on rock, but on unstable soil that couldn't resist the winds and waves. Two thousand years ago, Jesus warned of what would happen if you build your house on shifting sand rather than rock. It's still true today.

After two millennia, who can forget the parable of the prodigal son in Luke 15?

Jesus also uses illustrations to convey the salient truths found in His final sermons. In John 10, Jesus paints Himself as the Good Shepherd and the Door of the sheepfold. He illustrates our relationship by saying, "The sheep hear my voice." He also goes on to warn against trying to gain entrance into the sheepfold by scaling the fence. To gain entrance to the enclosure through any other means than going through the door would brand one as a thief and a robber. This is a severe warning to anyone who would avoid going through Jesus, the only true door.

The minutes or seconds it took for Jesus to describe the scenario of the sheep, shepherd, and sheepfold provide mental images that will forever conjure up the love of the Shepherd for the sheep and the dangers inherent in being an imposter.

In John 15, Jesus describes Himself as the vine, His Father as the farmer, and the believers as the branches. I don't think any of us need additional explanation when He describes the pruning process. It seems painfully obvious.

Nearly two-thirds of the Gospels would be eliminated if we removed all the graphic pictures that Jesus used to illustrate His point. It would serve leaders well to follow Jesus' method and use examples and anecdotes when preaching and teaching.

Wouldn't it be nice for people to remember what you said even after you're no longer on this earth?

To this day, people use biblical illustrations to prove their point. In one of Abraham Lincoln's famous speeches, he quoted Jesus' famous words, "A house divided against itself cannot stand" to help his hearers picture the ultimate devastation of the Civil War should the nation become divided (Mark 3:25). (The speech is even called the "House Divided" Speech.) Lincoln was a master at using metaphors to prove his point, including many that were from scripture.

Dr. Tony Campolo, the famous Christian sociologist and speaker, has some of the most memory-worthy illustrations ever. His messages, spoken before masses of youth in outdoor concert venues across the U.S., were not only mesmerizing, but deeply impactful, to the point of countless thousands of youth committing their lives to Jesus. I've personally used his illustrations dozens of times, always giving credit to Tony. It's amazing—though the stories can be retold hundreds of times, they still carry important graphic truths that makes them ageless. His message "It's Friday, But Sunday's Coming" will never be forgotten by me or anyone else who has heard him.

The same is true of Dr. Tony Evans, the pastor of Oak Cliff Bible Fellowship in Dallas, Texas, and countless other great speakers and preachers. What makes them truly great are the visual examples they insert into their messages that make them unforgettable. Dr. Evans is a brilliant theologian and scholar, with amazing oratorical skills, but what makes his messages so outstanding are the poignant stories he includes that helps make the sermon unforgettable.

Another Evans, Jimmy Evans, founder of Marriage Today, is one of my favorite speakers and preachers of all time. Next to his wife and Jesus, I'm positive I'm his biggest fan. I love Jimmy. What makes Jimmy's teaching so powerful is that at every conference he speaks at, he uses himself and his wife Karen as an example. I've heard Jimmy speak for decades and I can tell his story nearly as well as he can. Not only are they good examples of what to do and what not to do, but the mental image Jimmy paints will stay with you for a lifetime, continuing to bear fruit in your marriage. That is much better than hearing a sermon that is easily forgotten.

Less Is More

Minutes before Dr. Martin Luther King, Jr. made his famous seventeen-minute speech on the Washington Mall in 1963, the famous gospel singer, Mahalia Jackson, encouraged him to put away his pages of notes and tell the people his dream. "I Have a Dream" became one of the most memorable speeches ever delivered in the history of mankind. Thank God Mahalia didn't encourage him to give three salient points relating to people's social, racial, and spiritual needs. If he had done that, within minutes no one would have remembered what he said. As it is, no one at the event or since will ever forget what Martin Luther King, Jr. said. He etched in our minds the picture of racial equality in America and inspired us all to *dream big* in that regard.

As an aside, Martin Luther King's speech lasted only seventeen minutes at the March on Washington in 1963. One hundred years earlier, in 1863, President Abraham Lincoln's speech at the dedication of the Soldier's National Cemetery in Gettysburg, Pennsylvania, famously known as the Gettysburg

Address, lasted only a few minutes. On the same occasion as Lincoln's address, the politician Edward Everett spoke, with an oration that rambled on for more than two hours. Do you get the point? The more you talk, the less people will remember. The less you speak, the more likely they will remember both the speech and you. In my opinion, most sermons and speeches are much too long. I would rather speak just a few minutes and leave people wanting more than to talk too long and leave them with the lasting memory of "Ugh, that was painful!"

A Picture Is Worth a Thousand Words

In 1972, I had the privilege of attending teaching sessions by the world-renowned humanitarian and speaker, Corrie ten Boom, the legendary survivor of the Nazi Holocaust. She and her family were charged with rescuing Jewish families from death at the hands of their Nazi captors. Corrie was the only survivor in her family.

I sat directly in front of her as she taught at the tiny village of Hurlach, outside of Munich, Germany. A thousand Youth With A Mission (YWAM) evangelists, including fifty from my church, were evangelizing the streets of Munich during the Summer Olympics. Every other day we would stay behind at the Schloss Hurlach and be taught by Corrie and other well-known speakers.

On one particular morning, Corrie spoke about God's plan for our lives. To press her point that His plan may not make sense at the time, she made clear that if we will await the timing of God, we will see His special purpose fulfilled in us.

In the middle of her message, she brought out a small, framed tapestry. It was pathetically woven, unmatched in the color scheme, and with no apparent design. She described our lives as being like that. It doesn't make sense, and things happen to us for no apparent reason. Long stretches of nothingness are rarely broken by any circumstance that seems to advance our situation. My immediate thought was, "Corrie, you need to stick to your day job, speaking to people. You're much better at that than weaving tapestries."

After spending several minutes showing how God has a specific plan for our lives, she turned the tapestry over, revealing a gorgeous pattern. Now everything made sense. She had been showing us the backside. There appeared to be no design, no apparent plan, nothing that would indicate that a quality tapestry existed, until she turned it over. Messages, sermons, and orations, no matter how profound, cannot be fully described until someone "turns it over" with a visual anecdote or illustration.

That was in 1972 and I've never forgotten it. I never will. My life has had all kinds of turns, stops, skips, bumps, injuries, joys, disappointments, fears, and failures. The colors haven't always made sense. The crisscrossing of threads has been unclear to me. God brought people into my life, then took them out. Trials came. I struggled for purpose in life. Even God didn't make sense. Nothing made sense. Only when God finishes the tapestry will it all make sense. For so much of my life, I looked at the backside of the tapestry. All the while, God knew the end from the beginning and had planned my purpose with picture-perfect clarity.

Unless you paint mental pictures to convey your message, it is guaranteed to be lost, having wasted the time of the speaker

Only when God finishes the tapestry will it all make sense.

and audience. Why should I take 30-45 minutes of people's time only to have it forgotten within minutes after they leave the sanctuary? Yet that happens in congregations regularly throughout the world every Sunday.

If you can't think of effective illustrations, the Old Testament is replete with them. Try painting pictures from biblical examples. They worked for the New Testament writers; they will also work for you.

After I had graduated from high school, my mother and dad began traveling as itinerant evangelists, preaching in churches across America. My dad was a terrible speaker, so we tried to keep him out of the pulpit as much as possible so as not to embarrass him. But what he lacked in oratorical skills he made up for in love. He loved people so fervently that nearly every day of the week he led someone to the Lord. When dad passed away, the ribbon over dad's casket said it all: "Mr. Soulwinner." He truly was. It was my mom, however, who was the preacher, and she was really, really good. In the days when women preachers were scorned, mom, because of her incredible anointing, had no lack of churches to preach in.

My mother deserved at least a master's degree, if not a doctorate, in the use of illustrations that made her sermons unforgettable. People remembered them for decades. In preparing her messages, she would always search for her illustrations first. Much like African-American pastors have done throughout history, she brought Old and New Testament stories to life, then connected them to salient current truths. Then she wove in personal illustrations that sealed the deal. Her messages were poignant, powerful, and unforgettable. She didn't have three, five, or ten points; she had only one point, and man did she ever make it. She piqued our interest, zeroed in on our issues as well as her own, and left us with an indelible mental and moral image of how God wants us to live.

I recently listened to three of her messages given in 1985 at Christian Assembly Church in Peoria, Illinois. I didn't even know they existed.[1] We gathered our office staff together and showed a portion of one of her messages. I heard the staff continue to discuss for days the illustration she gave from the prophecy of Joel and Micah, of how she beat her "sword into a plowshare" (the cutting blade of a plow), meaning how God changed her temperament and tongue from the sword of destructive anger to an instrument of growth.

The illustration she used was how she and dad would come into their hotel room following a church service and routinely hang up their clothes. In this particular hotel room, there was little closet space, so both of them would use a hook on the back of the door to hang their evening clothes. The only problem was that my dad preferred hanging his coat over the hook, rather than using a coat hanger, making it impossible for additional clothes to be hung on the hook.

After telling my dad multiple times to please not put his coat over the hook, she came in one night to find he had again hung his coat over the hook. Obviously, Dad felt it

1. I'm not sure you can still view them, but we watched them on YouTube.

more convenient to do it his way. That was the last straw. She promptly threw his coat on the floor. When dad came in, he immediately picked it up with the comment: "Oh, look, my coat has fallen onto the floor." "No, honey, your coat didn't fall onto the floor, I threw it there. And I stepped on it too."

In the middle of the night, my mom repented to dad, providing an illustration of how God wants to change our temperament and tongue from a sword of destruction to the plowshare of productivity. As the crowd roared in knowing laughter over mom's intemperance, they also got the point, not of the sword, but of the plowshare.

One pastor introduced my wife, Devi, by saying, "She is the daughter-in-law of Rachel Titus. How many people remember what Rachel Titus preached on twelve years ago?" Hands shot up across the sanctuary. Twelve years ago. I can think of no greater compliment than for people to remember my messages over a decade after I'm gone. Remember, people characteristically remember a sermon for only five minutes after the delivery. That means they have most likely forgotten the message by the time they exit the front door of the church, but twelve years later? Powerful! Unforgettable.

Your Story Is Your Greatest Tool

When I was in college, my public speaking teacher taught that one should never use a personal illustration or refer to themselves while giving a speech. In hindsight, that is the dumbest advice I've ever heard. What better way to emphasize a point than to use an illustration from your own life? Your past is a poignant reminder, whether good or bad, of what you experienced, as well as a visual example to your audience of what should or should not be done.

When Jesus spoke to the woman of Samaria, He used her personal life as the entry point for His message. "Come, see a man who told me everything I ever did," she told people afterwards (John 4:29 NIV). What was the result? The entire town came out to see Jesus, and many believed in His name. That's one effective message.

Your testimony is a powerful tool in introducing people to Jesus in a touching, visual, and often emotional way. Don't be afraid to use it, or anything else that will bring home a point. An illustration is a powerful way of driving home a point, even if it is yours. After all, what better expert about a subject than the person who experienced it first-hand?

My Life as an Illustration

In 1980, I went through the deepest trial of my life. I nearly lost everything. It was deeply humiliating. I was filled with shame and remorse. For months I wouldn't tell anyone what I had been through. Then one day, while speaking on Philippians 3:10-11 at a church in Decatur, Illinois, I heard the Holy Spirit say, "Illustrate that verse with your own story." I was mortified. *You're kidding. I can't tell anyone that story. It's too painful*, I thought.

To remind you of what Philippians 3:10-11 says, Paul describes the essence of his passion for Jesus by declaring, "That I may know him and the power of his resurrection, and may share his sufferings, becoming like him in his death, that by any means possible I may attain the resurrection from the dead."

The World's Greatest Leader used pictures to illustrate his point.

To illustrate this verse from my own life, I told them my testimony of what happened to me in the winter of 1980. I summarized my pain, persecution, death to pride, and ultimately the loss of almost everything. My wife and children were with me, but we lost our home, church, reputation, and any hope for a successful future. To my surprise, instead of the congregation rejecting my message, they began to cry. Hours of preaching and numerous points couldn't have accomplished what was done in mere minutes through the use of my personal story. It actually became a point of healing, not only for me, but for the congregation as well.

The same thing happened several years later in Nigeria when I faced a very hostile group of pastors. Because of a disagreement the leaders were having with the pastor, half of them liked me and the other half had already decided they didn't. Rather than address the factious issues, I decided to tell them my story. By the time I got to the end of my testimony, the friction in the room had dissolved and my heart had meshed with theirs.

Everyone has a personal story. The Bible calls it a testimony. If you can't find anything else to share, share what God has done and is doing in your life. Revelation 12:11 says the persecuted saints in the end times overcame by the blood of the Lamb and the word of their testimony. You will not only fuel the imagination of your audience, but you'll let them know that they can go through the trial too.

If you connect only with people's intellects and not their imaginations, they will effectively forget what you said. The World's Greatest Leader used pictures to illustrate His point.

Before you preach your next sermon or give your next speech, I would recommend you prayerfully consider how you might stimulate the imagination of the hearers by including a salient illustration, so people will never forget the point you're trying to make. To *lead differently* you must speak differently. To speak differently you must use illustrations.

Good leaders speak differently to make a difference.

CHAPTER 9

Lead
by waiting for
right timing

*Observe due measure, for right timing is
in all things the most important factor.*

Hesiod, Greek didactic poet

(c. 800 BC)

*"But they who wait for the Lord shall renew their
strength; they shall mount up with wings like eagles; they
shall run and not be weary; they shall walk and not
faint."*

Isaiah 40:31

My daughter, Trina, recently told me a story about a conversation she had several years ago with her son, Brandon, during a very difficult time in her life. "Brandon, please pray and agree with me. I'm desperate for a breakthrough." She had gotten so weary of the trial she was going through, she wanted it to end immediately. She wanted Brandon to agree with her for a "breakthrough," now! Brandon's reply was classic: "Mom, you need to pray for patience." Ouch!

Patience is the ability to wait on God's timing before proceeding with a course of action.

Solomon was the wisest man on earth. He said, *"For everything there is a season, and a time for every matter under heaven"* (Ecclesiastes 3:1).

Solomon was trying to tell us that timing is everything! Timing is at the heart of God, and we see Him more clearly as we recognize His modulation of time in our lives. In fact, even if something is in God's will, unless it corresponds to His timing, He won't sanction it. If we insist on doing things in our own timing, the consequences can be catastrophic. Our leadership authenticity will evaporate and trust we've earned will vanish.

God's timing and our timing are not read from the same clock. If you want to be reminded of an excellent example of "God Time" vs. "Man Time," let's go back over the story of Abraham, the father of our faith.

Abraham Couldn't Wait

When Abraham was 75 years old, God called him out of Ur of the Chaldeans. In Genesis 15, God promised Abraham

> Patience is the
> ability to wait on
> God's timing before
> proceeding with a
> course of action.

that He would give him a son, even though his wife, Sarah, was barren.

Unwilling to wait for the son of promise, Isaac, Abraham made one of the biggest mistakes known to humanity. He fathered a son through his servant Hagar, completely ignoring God's promise and timing. In his attempt to do God's will in his own timing, he created a disaster that has lasted for millennia.

Hundreds of thousands of people have been caught in a conflict that continues to this day, all because of Abraham's unwillingness to wait on the promise of God. The Arab nations, descendants of Ishmael, have been in constant battle with the sons of Isaac, the Jewish people, for over four thousand years. In modern times, the peace talks between Israel and the Palestinians have continued for decades, regardless of how many nations, presidents, or diplomats try to intervene. It's really hard, if not impossible, to undo a rash decision.

Finally, when Abraham was 99 years old, God confirmed His promise to him. When he was 100 years old and Sarah was 90, she conceived and gave birth to Isaac, the son of the promise.

When there is a span of twenty-five years between the time of the promise and the time of the fulfillment, our intemperate and impatient natures stand up to help God by rushing the process. But I've never found God to be cooperative. No one can rush God, not even Abraham. God has a master plan that everyone must conform to, even though they might have received a valid promise, revelation, or prophetic word from God.

In the Fullness of Times

Jesus knew that God had a select time for everything and that God cannot be rushed. He also knew that if He missed the Father's timing, He would also miss His will. It was in the fullness of times that God sent His Son (Galatians 4:4). Everything must sync with the Father's intention and follow the score He has written.

Consider these magnificent historical events and how God orchestrated their precise flow:

- The angel Gabriel was sent by God to Zechariah, the father of John the Baptist, at the exact day and hour he was chosen (out of thousands of other priests) to burn incense on the Golden Altar (Luke 1:5-25).
- Six months after Gabriel was sent to Zechariah, he was again dispatched by God to notify the virgin Mary of the birth of the Son of God. The announcement, when made by Mary to Elizabeth, brought the prophetic

response of the baby John being filled with the Holy Spirit in Elizabeth's womb (Luke 1:26-56).

- The Roman Emperor, Caesar Augustus, had to give the census decree at the precise time for Mary and Joseph to return from Nazareth to their ancestral home so Jesus could be born in Bethlehem, fulfilling biblical prophecy in Micah 5:2.

- The stars had to align perfectly to guide the astrologers in their long journey from Persia, arriving at the precise time of Jesus' birth (Matthew 2).

- The room in the inn had to be too crowded to allow for extra guests so Joseph's family would be forced to stay in the stable, God's preference for the delivery room. It was in God's plan that the one sent from heaven as God incarnate would be wrapped in birthing cloths and placed in an animal feeding trough (Luke 2:7; 2 Corinthians 8:9).

- The announcement of Jesus' birth was given to Bethlehem shepherds who were protecting the lambs that would eventually be slain as a sacrifice for sin during the Passover (Luke 2:8-15).

- The *Pax Romana*, the peace the Roman Empire provided, produced the political environment for the Gospel to be spread throughout the known world.

- The Greek language was the *lingua franca* that made the Gospel accessible to all people and would also be the language in which the New Testament would be written.

- Jesus had to be born during the reign of Herod the Great, who, fearing a usurper to his throne, issued the decree to kill all the male children under two years of age so the prophecy of Rachel crying inconsolably for her children could be fulfilled (Jeremiah 31:15).

- Jesus had to be taken to Egypt as a child to fulfill the scripture which prophesied that the Messiah would come out of Egypt (Hosea 11:1; Matthew 2:13-15).

- Jesus' family had to live in Nazareth so the prophecy of Isaiah 11:1 would be fulfilled that the Messiah would be called a Nazarene (Matthew 2:19-23).

- Jesus had to begin His ministry in Capernaum so the prophecy would be fulfilled, "The land of Zebulun and the land of Naphtali . . . have seen a great light" (Matthew 4:15-16; Isaiah 9:1).

- Jesus had to be crucified at the exact time it was prophesied in Daniel, that the *"anointed one"* would be "cut off" (crucified) after He had made atonement for sin, on April 3, AD 33. This prophecy was given by Daniel 604 years before Christ (Daniel 9:26).

- Jesus had to die by the hands of the Romans through the horrible punishment of crucifixion to fulfill several Old Testament prophecies of the Messiah as the Suffering Servant (Isaiah 53; Psalm 22).

- Jesus had to die at Passover to fulfill His Messianic destiny as the Lamb of God to fulfill the Jewish feast of *Pesach* (Leviticus 23:4-5).

- Jesus had to rise again on the first day of the week to fulfill the Jewish Feast of First Fruits (Leviticus 23:9-11).

- The Holy Spirit had to be sent on the Day of Pentecost to coincide with the giving of the Law at Sinai (Exodus 19; Leviticus 23:15-21; Acts 2:1-4).

Furthermore, I have every reason to believe Jesus will return at the blowing of the trumpets announcing *Rosh Hashanah*, the first fall feast of the Jewish calendar (Leviticus 23:23-25; 1 Thessalonians 4:16; 1 Corinthians 15:52). Thus far Jesus has fulfilled each of the Jewish festivals, so why would His return be any different? The Sabbath between *Rosh Hashanah* and the Day of Atonement (*Yom Kippur*) is called *Shabbat Shuvah* by the Jews, meaning the Sabbath of Return. Paul says that Jesus' return would be preceded by the sounding of the trumpet (1 Thessalonians 4:16; 1 Corinthians 15:52). Everything God does is timed. *You cannot know God's will without conforming to His timing.* Learn to wait on the Lord.

Trying to Rush God

I've missed God's timing on numerous occasions. I've jumped out of the boat before I even knew if it was Jesus walking on the water! And as I was "glub, glub, glubbing" to the bottom of the lake, I would admit that maybe—just maybe—I might have been looking at my clock rather than the Father's. It's amazing what water in your lungs can teach you. Have you ever missed it? Well, you're in good company. Learn to wait on the Lord. It's an invaluable lesson.

I can't tell you the number of times that I have misjudged God's timing, generally by rushing it. Occasionally I'm behind God, moving too slowly when He speaks, but that is rare. It's also rare for most Christians. The majority of Christians attempt to rush God into moving, unwilling to wait for His timing, only to discover, to their regret, that He can't be rushed. I'm also convinced that Satan is behind many of these false starts by whispering in our ears, "Go ahead. You don't want to miss your opportunity." He also throws in an unhealthy dose of anxiety to push us into premature action. One of Satan's most strategic tools is to push us to rush our decisions.

My daughter, Trina, says that God will provide all of your needs if you're willing to wait. I think she's right. Rarely are things absolutely not God's will, especially when requested by one of His children. But our impatience often aborts God's plan and our desire.

How many marriages have ended tragically because couples were unwilling to wait for the right one? Or when things got tough, instead of honoring their marriage vows, they abruptly terminated the marriage? We rarely stop to think of the negative consequences that will most likely occur because of our impulsiveness, including possible long-term trauma to our children.

In John 7, Jesus' biological half-brothers prodded Him to go to the Feast of Tabernacles so He could "show off" His miraculous powers. Not only did He refuse to be moved by their impatience, but He also chided them for their insensitivity to the will of God. "My time has not yet come, but your time is always here" (John 7:6). I don't know if you caught it, brothers, but that wasn't a compliment. You have such little discernment about God's timing it really doesn't matter when you go, but for Jesus His Father's timing was a big deal. It should be a "big deal" to us as well.

Jesus' mother made the same mistake at the Cana wedding, but received, however, a milder rebuke: "Woman, what does this have to do with me? My hour has not yet come" (John 2:4). Fortunately, He didn't leave her in an entirely bad light. Producing 150 gallons of wine would brighten anyone's spirits.

If you're out of God's timing, you're out of His will, period!

The Holy Spirit didn't come whenever He chose, but He waited fifty days after the Passover to make His presence known. Many scholars believe this waiting period coincided perfectly with the giving of the Law on Mt. Sinai. The children of Israel arrived at the foot of the mountain exactly fifty days after leaving Egypt. Approximately 1,400 years later, the fire would again fall, but this time in the Upper Room, and the mountain would be Mt. Zion.

The disciples, likewise, were instructed by Jesus to wait in Jerusalem until the Day of Pentecost had fully arrived. Everyone had to show up at the same time, on the right day, at the right hour, at the exact location for the Holy Spirit to make His arrival.

Everything God does is according to timing. Thank God the days of creation weren't messed up. What if God had made the vegetation prior to the light, the birds before the atmosphere, the cattle before the straw, or the fish before the oceans?

For those who desire to be great leaders in God's kingdom, you must learn to move only when the Spirit prompts you; otherwise you will be out of God's will. In fact, you must *practice* doing this. If you're out of God's timing, you're out of His will, period! "Timing is everything" is more than a cliché; it's an absolute truth. The promise of God is for those who "wait for the Lord" (Isaiah 40:31).

Rash decisions also have an earthly effect. Moving unadvisedly and preemptively can cause people to not take you seriously. Impulsiveness is not uncommon in immature people, but constantly rushing to make decisions can destroy your credibility. It's not just a matter of, "Grow up, will you?" but it's a more serious matter of, "Can I really trust you?" Without maturity, leadership can devastate and disenfranchise.

Have you heard of the infamous second lieutenant in the military? This junior officer frightens his command because of his tendency to make decisions that cost lives. If you're a new and lightly-experienced leader, recognize your need to use maturity and be deliberate in your decisions! Everything in life demands perfect timing.

The Value of Waiting

Isaiah 40:30-31 says, "Even youths shall faint and be weary, and young men shall fall exhausted; but they who wait for the LORD shall renew their strength; they shall mount up with wings like eagles; they shall run and not be weary; they shall walk and not faint."

Psalm 38:15 reveals the heart of David: "But for you, O LORD, do I wait." In David's case He had to endure the persecution of Saul and years of being chased around in the wilderness before God would promote him to the throne. You could say that David was "practiced in the art of waiting." Had David not waited, the character, humility, and experience he needed to rule a nation would never have developed. As it was, the angel Gabriel announced that the coming Messiah, Jesus Christ, would sit on "the throne of his father, David" (Luke

1:32). That's a pretty good reward for waiting. If you ask me, it was worth the wait.

Micah also had the wisdom to wait until he heard from God. Micah 7:7 says, "But as for me, I will look to the LORD; I will wait for the God of my salvation; my God will hear me."

Isaiah 30:18 declares, "Therefore the LORD waits to be gracious to you, and therefore he exalts himself to show mercy to you. For the LORD is a God of justice; blessed are all those who wait for him."

If Israel had chosen to cross the wilderness before the pillar of cloud or fire moved, they would have lost their air conditioner during the day and their heater during the night. That's not a good idea. Sunburn is a terrible thing and so is frostbite; it's better to move only when God does. You will always make camp with Him if you move in the secure safety of His intention and timing.

Consider these examples of waiting on God:

- Jesus had to wait thirty years before He was baptized in the water and Spirit, and the Father spoke, validating Him and releasing Him into ministry (Luke 3:23).
- Moses had forty years of waiting in the wilderness before he experienced the burning bush, then more waiting before encountering the burning mountain (Acts 7:30).
- Thirteen years after Joseph had his first dream, God released him from prison and promoted him to the rulership of Egypt (Genesis 37:2; 41:46).
- Abraham waited twenty-five years from God's promise to make him a great nation until Sarah gave birth to Isaac, the son of promise (Genesis 12:1-4; 21:5).

In these examples and many more, the intended result would never have happened had they not waited. Our impatience never causes God to change His mind.

I Want Patience and I Want It Now!

I once heard a person say in jest, "I want patience and I want it right now." But for me it was never a jest. It's always been one of the biggest challenges of my life. Waiting has never been easy. That is part of the tempering process for leadership, isn't it? God gives you the passion and urgency to lead others. But He also carefully cools the steel in just the right way to forge you into a stronger implement. Leaders . . . learn to wait.

I remember as a kid not wanting to wait until the seed germinated. It was a class project that everyone would plant a seed, water it for weeks, and then eventually a little fleck of green would begin poking out through the soil. But as usual, I was impatient. I couldn't wait, so I'd dig it up to see how it was doing. Of course, that killed it.

If you crack open the cocoon too soon, the butterfly will never fly.

If you remove the cake from the oven before it's sufficiently baked, it will be ruined; the texture doesn't change, it stays gooey in the middle, it doesn't rise, and the cake falls. Can you blame people for not wanting to eat your cake? Can you fault people when they don't want to follow you because your plans are half-baked?

Notice, in John 7:30, the people were seeking to arrest Jesus, but no one laid a hand on Him, "because his hour had not yet come." It should be greatly encouraging to know that God's plans for your life can never be derailed by demonic activity or satanic intrusion contrary to God's will. He won't allow it. God has a perfect plan for your life, and when it's in His timing, it will come to pass. But there is no guarantee that God will follow through on His plans when you fail to wait for His timing.

The Apostle Paul makes clear in Philippians 1:6 that God "who began a good work in you will bring it to completion at the day of Jesus Christ." You can count on it. I don't know the day or the hour, but God will complete what He began. Relax and wait.

A friend of mine from Nepal was imprisoned for fourteen years because of his preaching of the Gospel. While incarcerated in the last of the three prisons in which he was held, the Holy Spirit told him the year, month, day, and hour he would be released. Many months ahead, he informed the inmates of when God would release him. They were obviously incredulous. While some rejoiced, most of them scoffed. Months later, on the exact month, day, and hour, at precisely 12 o'clock noon, his captors came and released him. There were more than a few men who surrendered their lives to Jesus that day as he exited the prison. God is never late in His timing.

Joshua's Timing

God told Joshua to march around Jericho for six days, then on the seventh day to march around it another seven times (Joshua 6). Frankly, I'm glad I wasn't an Israelite on that day. I would have probably jumped out of line on the sixth day. If

I had made it to the seventh day, I would have encouraged a mutiny. "Why can't we blow the trumpets now? Why do we have to wait? I'm sick and tired of going in circles around this dumb city." "Anybody got a trumpet? Let's start the party now."

That's why I was never good at baseball. I was unwilling to wait until it could be clearly seen that the ball was crossing the plate. As soon as it was thrown, I'd start swinging.

In the book *What to Do When It's Your Turn (and it's always your turn)*, Seth Godin says, "Please, wait. Let it simmer. It might not be for you, but at least this time, postpone the relief of resolution. This is your opportunity to make something that matters." I love his description of the "relief of resolution." Something inside us is so impatient for things to be resolved. We're always in a rush to "make it happen," and then we are disappointed or even devastated when it doesn't.

Author and motivational speaker Dan Millman said, "I learned that we can do anything, but we can't do everything . . . at least not at the same time. So think of your priorities not in terms of what activities you do, but when you do them. Timing is everything."

I love the comment by the famous baseball player, Yogi Berra, which I obviously didn't follow: "You don't have to swing hard to hit a home run. If you got the timing, it'll go."

Olympic athlete, Carl Lewis, agrees: "Life is about Timing."

Former Canadian Prime Minister, Pierre Trudeau, evidently feels the same way about politics: "The essential ingredient of politics is timing."

Waiting on God

Thank God for my wife, Devi. She's my ballast, emergency brakes, and wisdom when I'm rushing in where angels fear to tread. She forces me to slow down, go back over the realities and facts, take time to rehearse my decisions, and check my motives. She's really much better at timing than I am. I'm impulsive, spontaneous, and rarely count the cost. She does all of the above and carefully checks every decision box.

In 2002, I felt the Lord speaking to me that we were to move to Dallas, Texas from Ohio. I shared with Devi what I sensed God wanted us to do. I had logical reasons why we should move, such as the benefits of living closer to an international airport and to our daughter's family who lived there, but the bottom line was I felt I heard from God. When a person pulls out the "I heard from God" trump card, most people cave in and delay or remove their cautions. After all, who can argue with God? But not Devi. That didn't convince her in the least.

Devi too felt that we should move to Texas, but the timing wasn't right. "Honey, I don't think we should move until we sell our house. If we don't sell our house, it would create a lot of difficulties for us that aren't necessary." Fortunately, this time I agreed with her and settled down for our house to sell. I thought it might take a few weeks or months before I could call the moving van. Man was I wrong. We waited, waited, waited, waited, and waited. I was ready to blow the trumpet after the first year. Finally, three years later, our house sold. Hum?

The timing could not have been more perfect. Every single detail fell into place. Even the beautiful home we were to eventually purchase wasn't available at the time I wanted to move. In fact, it sat empty for two whole years, bringing the price down to a level we could afford. God's timing is always perfect. If I'm willing to wait, God will always move on my behalf. If there's anything I've learned, it's that God won't be rushed. His ways are perfect.

I'm still waiting for the Dallas Cowboys football team to win another Super Bowl. It must not be God's timing. Anybody got a trumpet?

If you want to *lead differently*, you'll have to learn to wait.

CHAPTER 10

Lead
with knowledge
of the Word

*Education is useless without the Bible. The Bible was
America's basic textbook in all fields. God's Word,
contained in the Bible, has furnished all necessary rules to
direct our conduct.*

Noah Webster

*"And beginning with Moses and all the Prophets, he
explained to them what was said in all the Scriptures
concerning himself."*

Luke 24:27 NIV

I can just hear someone say, "Well, of course He knew the Word, He *was* the Word." But Paul is clear, in Philippians 2:6-8, that when Jesus became incarnate, He laid aside His privileges of Deity and limited Himself to only those things mankind is capable of doing and experiencing. Hebrews says that Jesus had to be like His brothers in every respect (Hebrews 2:17).

When Jesus clothed Himself in flesh, the flesh made demands of Him. The Bible says He became tired, He thirsted, He fell asleep on a fishing boat, His spirit was troubled, He cried, He was tempted, He became angry, and He was at times disappointed in the response of the disciples. Likewise, if He was a carpenter, splinters would have penetrated His flesh on many occasions. In learning the trade, it is inevitable that at times the hammer would miss the nail and hit His fingernail. And, in Jesus' day, carpenters were also well-trained as stone masons. Do you think Jesus might have dropped a rock on His foot a time or two? How it is possible to be a carpenter or stone mason without occasional painful accidents?

According to Luke 2:51, Jesus had to submit to the authority of His parents. An equally telling phrase is that Jesus "grew in wisdom and stature, and in favor with God and man" (Luke 2:52 NIV). If Jesus had to grow physically like everyone else, wouldn't it be plausible to think He also had to grow mentally like everyone else? To think otherwise would defy the whole purpose of Jesus becoming man, so He could die for mankind.

If Jesus grew mentally, then His knowledge of the Word would have been gained through study and memorization like everyone else. I don't believe that Jesus had some type of extra, supernatural perception, allowing Him to know the Word through spiritual osmosis or telepathy. If Jesus learned the Word through a natural process, which is the only biblical possibility, then it's obvious that we can be as educated in the Word as was Jesus. This appears to be what happened when He was twelve years of age.

Our first and only glimpse of Jesus as a child finds Him in the temple asking and answering questions in the company of the teachers of the Law (Luke 2:41-52).

So what were they discussing? Fishing in the Galilee? Roman politics? Carpentry? More than likely they were embroiled in wringing out truths from the *Tanakh*, the Hebrew Old Testament.

Not only did Jesus know the scriptures well, but He quoted them often. In Luke 4:4, 8, and 12, Jesus quotes Deuteronomy 8:3, 6:13, and 6:16 to respond to the devil's evil suggestions. A few verses later, He quotes Isaiah 61:1-2 to validate His call into the ministry. In John 5:39, Jesus makes clear that in addition to John the Baptist, the Father, and the supernatural works, it was also necessary for the Word of God to validate His ministry. When the disciples asked Jesus the purpose of parables in His teaching, He quotes directly from Isaiah 6:9. Everything Jesus did was based on the Word of God, and He knew it well.

In the Sermon on the Mount, Jesus quotes from Exodus, Leviticus, and Deuteronomy, three of the books of the Law, the Hebrew *Torah* (Matthew 5-7). He then gives His own commentary on what they meant. On one occasion, Jesus questions an expert in the law and commends him when he comes up with the correct answer. The Larry Titus paraphrase of Luke 10:28 is, "You're a good student; you quoted Deuteronomy 6:5 and Leviticus 19:18 correctly. I would have given you an 'A' if you hadn't started justifying yourself."

> # Not only did Jesus know the scriptures well, but He quoted them often.

Jesus Spoke from the Scriptures

Rather than quote all the other "quotes" that Jesus made from the Old Testament, I will refer you to His post-resurrection conversation with the men on the road to Emmaus. This is one of the shortest and most profound narratives in the scriptures: "And beginning with Moses and all the Prophets, he explained to them what was said in all the Scriptures concerning himself" (Luke 24:27 NIV). There's nothing quite like having a Bible study in the Word taught by *The Word!* Imagine the wonder of it—men walking on a primitive road with Jesus, their hearts lit by the chain reactions of understanding, their minds whirling with the comprehensive knowledge of the Messiah both in prophetic scripture and current history.

Jesus expanded on the same theme later in the evening when He explained to the disciples everything He had earlier said to Cleopas and his companion, but this time included the Psalms as well. He then opened their minds so they could understand the scriptures (Luke 24:44-45).

I want you to stop and ponder this. For Jesus to open up the entire Old Testament and exposit all the verses that related to Himself must have exposed an enormous amount of scriptural knowledge. Uncovering Jesus in Psalms alone could have taken up more than an average evening.

When Jesus introduced the coming Holy Spirit, He said, "He will teach you all things and bring to your remembrance all that I have said to you" (John 14:26). How can the Holy Spirit bring to your remembrance things you have never memorized? Have you ever considered the fact that if Jesus memorized scripture, it might be a good idea for you too?

Knowing the Word Gives You Authority

A leader without an intimate knowledge of scripture lacks the authority to properly present the gospel message. It's not good enough to say, "It says somewhere." A "worker who does not need to be ashamed," must be one who "correctly handles the word of truth" (2 Timothy 2:15 NIV).

Of course, Paul knew the Word intimately.

The disciples knew the Word and quoted it often.

The Old Testament prophets knew the Word and quoted it to validate their prophecies.

Apollos, an early church leader, though a profound teacher of the Word, needed Priscilla and Aquila to explain it to him more thoroughly. As an aside, if anyone is interested in knowing who I think the author of the New Testament book of Hebrews is, I vote for Apollos. I personally don't believe it was Paul, but it had to be someone versed in the *Tanakh*, the Hebrew Old Testament. No one outside the Jerusalem circle of leaders, other than Timothy and Titus, was mentioned in the New Testament more often than Apollos.

> A leader without an
> intimate knowledge
> of scripture lacks the
> authority to properly
> present the gospel
> message.

Apollos was a Jew from Alexandria, "an eloquent man, competent in the Scriptures." "And when he wished to cross to Achaia, the brothers encouraged him and wrote to the disciples to welcome him. When he arrived, he greatly helped those who through grace had believed, for he powerfully refuted the Jews in public, showing by the Scriptures that the Christ was Jesus" (Acts 18:24, 27-28). Apollos sounds like an apologist to me—someone who could have authored the Book of Hebrews.

When I get to heaven, or when Jesus comes to earth to get me and all the saints, one of the first questions I want to ask Him is, "Who wrote the Book of Hebrews?" What do I get if I'm right, an extra jewel in my crown?

The power of God comes to a believer through prayer, but authority comes through your knowledge of the Word of God. Your emotions can never sustain you through life's exigencies and emergencies, much less prepare you to help others. Only the eternal Word of God can arm you with the weapons necessary to defeat the enemy as well as equip you and others to be victorious in life and eternity.

If Jesus, otherwise known as the Word of God (John 1:1, 14; Revelation 19:13), had to study and memorize the Word, how much more so do we, His followers, need to know the Word? A lack of knowledge of the Word will keep you immature and susceptible to the enemy's deceptions. Knowledge of the Word will provide the sword of the Spirit, which will both defeat Satan and make you powerful in Jesus' kingdom and church.

Wielding the Sword of the Spirit

There are only two weapons promised to the believer in Ephesians 6:12-18. The first is the sword of the Spirit, which is the Word of God, and secondly, prayer. Everything else— faith, truth, peace, righteousness, and other spiritual characteristics—are part of the believer's defense system. Your helmet of faith, breastplate of righteousness, sandals of peace, and loincloth of truth can never slay the enemy. Only the sword of the Spirit, the Word of God, can destroy the enemy. Neither can you be mature enough to wield this weapon without thoroughly knowing it. You can't throw a Bible at the devil; you have to do what Jesus did during the wilderness temptation: you have to quote it, understand it, and speak it with authority. "It is written" is a powerful tool to paralyze the enemy.

First Peter 4:11 says, "Whoever speaks, as one who speaks oracles [Greek *logos*, the word] of God."

My great fear is that in these last days the saints will be poorly prepared to face the massive onslaught of the enemy due to their lack of knowledge of the Word of God. They will also be susceptible to lying signs and wonders, doctrines of demons, and other trickeries of the deceiving spirits.

In 2 Corinthians 11:14-15, Paul describes the devil as an "angel of light," with his servants disguised as "servants of righteousness." It is obvious in the wilderness temptation that the devil knows the Word of God. He quotes from it three times from three different sources when accosting Jesus. The problem is that he takes it out of context, even adding to it, making it reinforce his interpretation.

How the Devil Distorts the Truth

In the Garden of Eden, Satan spoke from the mouth of the serpent. He distorted what God originally said.

Here is what God originally said:

> You may surely eat of every tree of the garden, but of the tree of the knowledge of good and evil you shall not eat, for in the day you eat of it you shall surely die. (Genesis 2:16-17)

These are the devil's words through the serpent:

> Did God actually say, "You shall not eat of any tree in the garden"? (Genesis 3:1)

No, God didn't say that at all. Plus, typical of the devil, he's casting God in a very negative light.

Every major cult is built on a distortion of the Word of God.

Since we're now on a roll, reinterpreting God's words to fit someone else's interpretation, let's see how Eve continued the distortion.

These are the woman's words:

> We may eat of the fruit of the trees in the garden, but God said, "You shall not eat of the fruit of the tree that is in the midst of the garden, neither shall you touch it, lest you die." (Genesis 3:2-3)

I can't find the phrase "neither shall you touch it" in God's words to Adam. The devil always deceptively adds to or takes away from sacred writ so it is no longer sacred and it's no longer God's Word.

Every major cult is built on a distortion of the Word of God. Many false doctrines start off with a kernel of truth, then add distortions until the entire belief system becomes untrue and dangerous. People lacking discernment buy into the deception. Had they known the pure Word of God in context, they could have foiled the enemy's attempt to delude and deceive them. As I heard several of my professors in Bible college say, a scripture taken out of *context* becomes a *pretext*. Any truth that becomes a mixture of truth and error doesn't become a partial truth; it loses all its veracity. It is 100% error!

Whoever said that ignorance is bliss is blithely unaware of the dangers of biblical ignorance. Not only can the devil quote scriptures to you, always twisting them to deceive you, but so can demons. Demons were aware that Jesus was the Son of the Most High God even before the disciples were (Luke 8:26-33).

James 2:19 says that even demons believe that God is one, a quotation from Deuteronomy 6:4. If demons can believe without becoming believers, I wonder if the same thing can happen to humans?

The Devil Is a Liar—and His Miracles Are Too

I believe we are in the last days. In these times, we will see lying signs, wonders, and miraculous stunts—all displayed by the devil. We must know the Word of God or we will be deceived. Look at the battle between the magicians of Egypt and Moses, recorded in Exodus 7-8.

Moses would perform a miracle, then the Egyptians would perform the same miracle.

Moses threw down his rod and it became a serpent. The magicians threw down their staffs and they too became serpents.

Moses turned the water of the Nile into blood, and so did the magicians.

A third Satanic miracle is recorded in Exodus 8:5-8:

> And the LORD said to Moses, "Say to Aaron, 'Stretch out your hand with your staff over the rivers, over the canals and over the pools, and make frogs come up on the land of Egypt!'" So Aaron stretched out his hand over the waters

> # I'm not impressed with any miracle, sign, or wonder unless it aligns with the Word of God and Jesus is glorified.

of Egypt, and the frogs came up and covered the land of Egypt. But the magicians did the same by their secret arts and made frogs come up on the land of Egypt.

For the first three supernatural demonstrations it was a tit-for-tat, with the magicians performing miracles to match those of Moses. When Moses got to the more powerful miracles, however, the magicians were forced to drop out. I believe the same will happen in the last days. The spiritual imposters will try to duplicate the miracles of the Holy Spirit, but they can only go so far. Only God can produce miracles that result in redemption.

Leaders must have a well-developed spiritual "lie detector" and call "false" when an illegitimate display of supernatural power happens. The ability to do so is based on knowing the Word.

In Revelation 14, in addition to the Antichrist, a second beast appears on the scene. Scripture calls this beast the false prophet, a powerful counterfeit parallel to the Holy Spirit. The false prophet is endowed with miraculous abilities to do great signs and wonders, causing people to worship the Antichrist. If you're impressed with the miraculous, you'll love this dude. The problem is that after they see signs and wonders, many people will turn to the Antichrist instead of to Jesus.

In Acts 8, Simon the Sorcerer amazed the Samaritans by his miraculous displays of power, until godly, Spirit-filled men exposed his subterfuge. Even his supposed conversion was suspicious and was exposed by Peter. Simon was evidently an example of someone who believed, but was not a believer.

When the disciples returned from one of their early missionary tours, in Luke 10, they rejoiced at how the enemy had been put to rout. Their rejoicing was short-lived, however, when Jesus interrupted their goose-bump stories with the abrupt statement, "All the same, the great triumph is not in your authority over evil, but in God's authority over you and presence with you. Not what you do for God but what God does for you—that's the agenda for rejoicing" (Luke 10:20 MSG).

I'm not impressed with any miracle, sign, or wonder unless it aligns with the Word of God and Jesus is glorified. To make sure that it does conform to the Word of God, I have to personally know the Word. Any authentic Christian leader must know the Word to promote sound doctrine and to protect those he teaches.

Years ago, a pastor wrote a book about angels and all the angelic visitations he was experiencing. People were mesmerized by his detailed descriptions of angels and how they were interacting with him. He drew huge crowds who were thrilled and chilled by these unusual heavenly visitors. The only problem was that he described angels doing things that were not biblical and gave them names not mentioned in the Bible. Angels are mentioned often in the Bible, but only two are named—Gabriel and the archangel Michael.

I began feeling uneasy about the whole thing. I didn't tell my congregation not to read the book. I encouraged them to read it with the Bible close at hand, comparing his experiences with what the Bible said. They discovered, through their own study, that the visitations were not of God. Wisdom demands that everything be filtered and compared with the Word of God. After the author's death, the whole angel frenzy vanished.

The Enemy's Circus Tricks

People are amazingly vulnerable to descriptions of the supernatural. In fact, we are like children when we hear of the spectral or the mythical. Most Christians desire to see the demonstration of the power of God, but let us be wary of the enemy's circus tricks.

In Matthew 7:21-23, the concluding verses of Jesus' Sermon on the Mount, He describes imposters who will try to gain entrance into the kingdom of God through their own piety, demonstration of spiritual gifts, displays of miraculous powers, or ability to exorcise demons. His response to them was, "I never knew you."

It is critical that we know the Word of God so that we're not swept away by the spiritual stage magicians of our day, unaware that the light and magic is not from God.

I'll say it again. (You know this is on my heart!) We must thoroughly know the Word of God in the last days, so we don't fall into the deception of the enemy. You don't have to be a seminarian to know the Bible. The Holy Spirit wrote the Bible so everyone could know and understand it. No academic degrees are necessary, just a hunger to know what God says through His Word.

The Copious Benefits of Reading the Word

I encourage you to read fewer books about what the Bible says and simply read more of the Bible. No matter how good other books are, books *about* the Bible don't have the credibility of the Bible itself. It is the infallible Word of God.

There are other reasons why you need to know the Bible:

- Psalms 119:11—It will keep you from sinning.
- Psalms 1—It produces maturity and prosperity.
- The entire Book of Proverbs gives insight into daily living.
- Matthew 24:35—It's eternal. It gives you security. Heaven and earth will pass away, but the Word won't pass away.
- John 1:1, 14—It reveals Jesus. Jesus is the Word. If you want to know Jesus, you must know the written Word.
- Psalms 119:105—It orders your steps, giving direction and clarity to your future.
- Psalms 119:130—It gives wisdom to the simple.
- Romans 10:17—It produces faith.
- Daniel 7, 9; Revelation 4-22—It reveals the future.

- Acts 8:4,14,25; 1 Peter 1:25; Romans 10:14-15—It is the Good News, the gospel, that is to be proclaimed throughout the world.
- 2 Peter 2:6-7—It reveals the judgment to come.
- Revelation 21-22—It reveals eternity and our eternal relationship with Jesus.
- Hebrews 4:12—It reveals the inner motives of a person's heart.
- Deuteronomy 6:7-9—It is the curriculum you should teach your children.
- 1 Timothy 4:13—It is the script that is to be read in public.
- Matthew 4:4—It will destroy the temptations of the enemy.
- John 5:24—It will give you eternal life.
- John 8:31—It will produce discipleship in you.
- Psalms 19:11—Obedience to the Word will provide a great reward for your future.
- John 17:17—It will sanctify you—set you apart in the truth.
- Isaiah 55:10-11—It accomplishes God's will on earth.
- Joshua 1:8—It will bring prosperity when you meditate on it.

The Founding Fathers Knew It Well

Virtually all of our Founding Fathers quoted copiously from the Bible. The Word was their authority to accomplish what they considered to be God's will. Noah Webster, known as the Schoolmaster of the Republic, said, "Education is useless without the Bible. The Bible was America's basic textbook in all fields of learning. God's Word, contained in the Bible, has furnished all necessary rules to direct our conduct."

In my opinion, the Second Inaugural Address of Abraham Lincoln, delivered on March 4, 1865, mere weeks before he was assassinated, is one of the greatest speeches ever written. In this short speech, Lincoln quotes three times from the Bible, twice from Matthew and once from Psalms. Lincoln had prolific knowledge of the Bible and used it often in his speeches. Years earlier, in a speech before the Illinois Republican Party, Mr. Lincoln quoted Jesus' famous words from Mark 3:25: "A house divided against itself cannot stand." This statement became the rallying cry for the anti-slavery Republicans and was also the basic theme for his presidency.

For Lincoln, who spent virtually every day of his presidency (1861-1865) embroiled in the Civil War conflict, there could not have been a better rock on which to anchor his convictions than the Word of God. Fortunately, he knew it well enough to quote it continually. There is no better authority than the Word of God. The Word of God is indeed the hammer that breaks the rock in pieces (Jeremiah 23:29). Ironically, Mark 3:25 is the same verse of scripture that Sam Houston proclaimed in the Senate eight years before the Civil War broke out. It was to become all too prophetic.

It has often been said that the Bible is more current than tomorrow's newspaper.

Because the Holy Spirit wrote the Bible, He also knows how to ignite it and unpack it in your heart. Isaiah 55:11 promises that the Word will never return void without accomplishing God's purpose. God sends the Word from heaven and it won't return to Him without causing growth. The men at the first post-resurrection Emmaus Road Bible study said that their hearts burned within them as Jesus opened the scriptures to their understanding.

Leaving a Legacy

As a child, I would walk the half-mile to school memorizing scriptures from the Bible. To this day, the Bible continues to give me life, insight, encouragement, wisdom, and direction. When the enemy comes in like a flood I can respond as Jesus did, "It is written," knowing that Satan is paralyzed when presented with the Word.

During the cold central California winter mornings of my childhood, I remember my dad with his feet propped up against the furnace reading the Bible. To this day, I recall my mother with her Bible on the kitchen table with ink, coffee, and tears having stained its well-worn pages. My family loves the Word. We live the Word. We speak the Word. We post the Word throughout our home. We have a plaque on the outside of our home, a Mezuzah, with the Word in it. In one painting alone, hundreds of scriptures crowd the framed masterpiece in our music room.

It was precisely because of the Word of God that John the Beloved received his monumental, life-changing revelation of Jesus Christ on the Isle of Patmos (Revelation 1:9). When you are full of the Word of God, you'll have a life-changing revelation of Jesus Christ too. You can only give out what you're full of. Make sure you're full of the Word of God. Leaders who *lead differently* know the Word, preach the Word, teach the Word, and live the Word.

CHAPTER 11

Lead
by seeking the
Kingdom first

*God's number one priority on earth is not the organized
Church but His Kingdom. The Church is who we are,
the Kingdom is what we do.*

Larry Titus

*"But seek first the kingdom of God and his righteousness,
and all these things will be added to you."*

Matthew 6:33

Devi and I began our first pastoral ministry in Wenatchee, Washington in 1968. We started off with a few dozen people. After one year, we still had a few dozen people. I was so frustrated! I did all I knew to do and experienced no success whatever. In fact, we were going backwards. Pretty soon, I thought, it will just be Devi, me, and our little daughter, Trina.

It was a warm spring day in the month of May when I laid down on the platform of our church and cried out to God in despair. "God, I've done all I know to do, and nothing works!" I lamented, immersed in self-pity. Poor me. *God, you've failed me. Again.*

Then I began to hear a voice. I don't know if others would have heard it, but my spirit clearly heard the voice of Jesus. I do not know how long it lasted. It might have been a half hour.

"Larry, do you ever preach on the kingdom of God?"

"No, Lord, I don't think I have."

"I always did."

"Do you ever preach on the church?"

"Oh, yes, Lord, I always do."

"I rarely did," was Jesus' response.

He then took me to Matthew 16:18, and the conversation continued: "Larry, I said that *I* would build *my* church. I didn't ask you to build my church; I said I would build it. I just asked you to build the kingdom of God."

The only times Jesus uses the word "church" are in Matthew 16 and 18. There is no further reference to the church by Jesus in any of the four Gospels.

As a reminder of what Matthew 16:18 says, I'll quote it here: "And I tell you that you are Peter, and on this rock I will build *my* church, and the gates of Hades will not overcome it" (NIV).

The second time Jesus mentions the word church, *ekklesia* in the Greek, is in Matthew 18:17, where He is advising brothers who have had friction between themselves. "If he refuses to listen to them, tell it to the church. And if he refuses to listen even to the church, let him be to you as a Gentile and a tax collector."

If Jesus didn't ask me to build the church, then my entire anxiety-filled year of laboring to build the church was totally unnecessary. I could have avoided all that worry. I was carrying an unnecessary load.

Like me, so many pastors have ministered faithfully through the years, trying to build the church that Jesus said He would build. Could that be you? It's a burden Jesus didn't ask you to carry.

I don't know if this was part of the conversation or not, but it's like I experienced an instant playback video of all the times I had invited people to "my" church, rather than Jesus' church. At that moment, "my church" became more than mere semantics. My selfish response exposed a depth of theological ignorance I had been unaware of. At that moment, deep conviction hit me that it's not "my" church but Jesus' church, and there's a big difference between the two!

Getting back to our one-way conversation, the Lord continued, "Larry, if you will build the kingdom of God, I will build the church." I had spent one year trying to build "my" church and failed miserably. If I had only realized God's purpose for me as a pastor was to build the kingdom of God, I could have avoided one year of effort totally void of the quickening of the Holy Spirit.

If Jesus rarely mentioned the word "church," what did He speak on? As you will soon see, there are nearly two hundred references made by Jesus to either the kingdom of heaven or the kingdom of God.

From the moment of that divine encounter, Devi and I began to devote all our efforts to building the kingdom of God, beginning with telling people about the King of the kingdom. I even stopped inviting people to church and instead told them how much Jesus loved them. And the funny thing is, our church building began filling up. Fast.

I vividly remember the first night we went into a tavern and began praying with people. I suffered from total self-consciousness. I was more concerned about who would see me in a bar than I was about witnessing to the people. We sat down at a table with a lady sitting by herself and looking lonely. As Devi and I talked, she set her drink aside and began to tell us her story. She had end-stage cancer. Within a few minutes, she responded to the message of Jesus' love and received Him as her Lord and Savior. Following this encounter, we stayed in touch with her and she died shortly thereafter.

We invited youth to our home and told them about Jesus. There were times when both levels of our split-level home were filled with youth, praying, receiving Christ, being delivered from demons, or being filled with the Holy Spirit.

We met them in restaurants and led them to Christ. We went to the local college and high school and told them about the love of God. We went to parks where youth gathered, sat down beside them as they smoked pot, and shared the love of God with them.

They didn't all come to our church, but within the first few years, over one thousand teenagers received Christ in one or more of our encounters. Then the parents began to come. We began to look for new facilities because our little 220-seat church could no longer accommodate the crowds of youth who were filling its aisles, pews, and even sitting on the floor.

They came in every form, flavor, and fashion. Drug dens emptied out as the kids were saved. The demon-possessed came. The disenchanted and disillusioned showed up. The outcasts timidly knocked on our door. The strung-out stumbled in. The religious kids who wanted more of Jesus appeared with questions. The scions of local civic leaders came. We even rented an empty historic home near the high school where the youth could stop by on their way home from school for prayer meetings and Bible studies. Some local churches weren't as excited about our success, but the youth sure were.

A high school student attending our church one day saw one of the high school kids in a main hallway of the school, totally strung out on drugs, sitting with his head between his knees. Soon this young man was led to Christ. He became one of our strongest leaders, later building a thriving church in the Seattle area that endures today.

When the church catches Jesus' view of the kingdom of God, the Holy Spirit shows up. The Spirit covers and empowers those with the vision, and phenomenal things begin to happen. I continually tell people, we need to take the church *out* of the church building and into the world, so you can *be* the church. The kingdom of God is what happens when you leave the confines of the church building; it is not what you do while you're there. The kingdom of God is what happens on Monday through Saturday.

If anyone questions Jesus' number one priority, all you have to do is read Matthew 6:33, found in His first sermon:

> # The church is who we are inside the building, and the kingdom is what we do out in the world.

Seek *first* the kingdom of God and his righteousness, and all these things will be added to you. (Matthew 6:33)

If you need additional proof, as I mentioned before, check out the number of times Jesus spoke on the kingdom of God as opposed to His references on the church, a lesson I'll never forget from my Jesus encounter that day many years ago.

Jesus spoke of the church only twice, Matthew 16:18 and 18:17, but there are nearly two hundred references in the Gospels to the kingdom of God or the kingdom of heaven. It was not that Jesus was understating the importance of the church, but instead emphasized that the church, His body, was the vehicle He would use to bring the kingdom to the hearts of the people.

Simply put, the church is who we are inside the building, and the kingdom is what we do out in the world.

The Bible, from beginning to end, is a kingdom book. In the Old Testament, many chapters are devoted to the kingdom of God, including chapters in Daniel, Isaiah, Ezekiel, and Zechariah. But what is introduced in the Old Testament is fully revealed in the New Testament, from Matthew all the way through the Book of Revelation.

The Kingdom of God Is at Hand

The first sermon John the Baptist preached was on the kingdom of God (Matthew 3:2). Not coincidentally, the first sermon Jesus preached was also on the kingdom of God (Matthew 4:17). In fact, His last sermon was on the kingdom of God as well. Acts 1:3 records what Jesus did following His resurrection and immediately before His ascension: "He presented himself alive to them after his suffering by many proofs, appearing to them during forty days and speaking about the *kingdom of God.*"

During His three and a half years of earthly ministry, Jesus traveled by foot from north to south in Israel, preaching in every town and village, speaking and proclaiming the kingdom of God (Matthew 4:23; 9:35). Did you catch that? In every single village and town where Jesus preached, His central topic was the kingdom. I don't know how many towns He preached in, but a quick perusal of the maps of Jesus' day shows that the number had to be large.

After being commissioned, the disciples expanded that number considerably. At the time I experienced my encounter with Jesus, I had never preached one message on the kingdom. Since then, I've preached on it hundreds of times in every nation, city, and church I've visited. It's also a main topic in conferences. If Jesus considered the kingdom of God so important, that must be my objective as well.

The Kingdom of God and the Kingdom of Heaven

In Matthew we find the term "kingdom of heaven," which is identical to the references in the remaining three Gospels where it says "kingdom of God." As many scholars believe, Matthew, writing exclusively to a Jewish audience, might have deliberately avoided the use of the sacred name for God for the more inclusive and less sensitive term, "heaven." The "kingdom of God" and the "kingdom of heaven" both refer to God's heavenly kingdom ruling over the kingdoms of this world.

Jesus refers to the kingdom of heaven in nearly every chapter in Matthew, and twelve times in chapter 13 alone. Notice that the majority of Jesus' parables were on the kingdom: Matthew 13:1-52; 20:1-16; 22:1-14; 25:1-13.

I can nearly hear one of the disciples in ancient Capernaum harping, "I know Jesus is going to come here too, but I get so tired of hearing the same old sermon, the kingdom of God, the kingdom of God, the kingdom of God. Doesn't He have something else to preach?" According to the Gospels, the answer was, "No, He didn't." Jesus was a one-topic preacher. It's obvious we wouldn't invite Him back to our churches more than once or twice. Who would come to hear someone who camped on the same topic every time?

The Practical Message

In truth, the gospel of the kingdom is the most practical message we can teach. Everything about the kingdom relates to the practicalities of how God reaches down to people, saves

> The gospel of the
> kingdom is the most
> practical message
> we can teach.

them, heals them, delivers them from Satanic oppression, and sets them free. Virtually all of Jesus' parables reflect His interest in seeing people's lives changed, now and for eternity.

In the early days of our Washington State experience, we learned that ministry included far more than initial salvation. The youth came out of the culture of drugs and hedonism into the kingdom environment of peace, life, and deliverance in Jesus. They were transformed from the kingdom of darkness to the kingdom of light. The devil's heavy yoke broke off them, replaced with Jesus' yoke of opposite proportions. "For my yoke is easy, and my burden is light," declares Jesus in Matthew 11:30. They discovered that Jesus' yoke was the opposite of their heavy yoke of sin.

One mother's concern prompted her to call me: "What's wrong with my son? He slept for nearly three days after he got religion." I didn't take the time to explain the difference between religion and true salvation. "There's nothing wrong with your son," I assured her. "This is the first time in his life he no longer carries a weight of guilt and shame." The kingdom of God had arrived, and with it came peace that surpassed understanding; his sleep was no longer troubled.

The Lord's Prayer

The most famous prayer in the world, universally referred to as the Lord's Prayer, begins with addressing the Father, then requesting, "Your *kingdom* come, your will be done, on earth as it is in heaven" (Matthew 6:10). Central in this detailed prayer is petitioning God for His kingdom to come and His will to be done on earth as it is in heaven.

Jesus establishes the priority of His mission a few verses later, when He turns His heavenly request into an injunction: "But seek *first* the kingdom of God and his righteousness, and all these things will be added to you" (Matthew 6:33). Now it's no longer just a request, but a priority. This is our first priority. *Heaven's will must become earth's reality*, brought by the believers' prayer and practice. On that fateful day in May, I made a decision to make God's priority mine, and I've never turned back.

More Than Prayer

In order to break the power of the kingdoms of this world and to establish God's heavenly will, we need to do more than pray. Jesus sent out the twelve disciples to *preach* on the kingdom as well (Matthew 10:7). Following the twelve, He commissioned the seventy to preach on the kingdom (Luke 10:9), and finally commissioned the early church, beginning at Pentecost (Acts 1:8).

Revealing the fact that the early church clearly pursued Jesus' mandate, Philip, one of the first deacons, preached the message of the kingdom to the segregated region of Samaria, and revival broke out.

> But now the people believed Philip's message of Good News concerning the Kingdom of God and the name of Jesus Christ. As a result, many men and women were baptized. (Acts 8:12 NLT)

Paul not only began his ministry preaching on the kingdom of God (Acts 14:22), but he ended it that way as well. "He lived there two whole years at his own expense, and welcomed all who came to him, proclaiming the kingdom of God and teaching about the Lord Jesus Christ with all boldness and without hindrance" (Acts 28:30-31).

I am convinced that true revival cannot be released until the glorious message of Jesus Christ and His kingdom goes forth from the four walls of the church, into the highways and byways of a desperate and hungry world. If Jesus commands us to *seek first the kingdom of God*," then church leaders, you must change your focus from building a church to building the kingdom. Amen?

The Kingdom Both Now and Later

So often we think of the kingdom of God as only futuristic, something that will happen when Jesus returns. But Jesus made it clear that the kingdom of heaven is at hand; it's as close as what you can reach out and touch. The kingdom of God is "NOW!"

In Luke 10:8-9, Jesus instructs the disciples, "When you enter a town and are welcomed, eat what is offered to you. Heal the sick who are there and tell them, 'The kingdom of God has come near to you'" (NIV).

I love the simplicity of The Message Bible: "When you enter a town and are received, eat what they set before you, heal anyone who is sick, and tell them, 'God's kingdom is right *on your doorstep!*'" That means it's as close as your front door.

What are some observable signs that the kingdom of God has arrived?

- When a person is healed or delivered from demons, the kingdom of God has appeared (Matthew 10:7-8; Luke 11:20).
- When anyone is born again, the kingdom of God has come (John 3:3, 5).
- When you feed the hungry, clothe the naked, visit the sick and imprisoned, you are granted the reward of the kingdom of God (Matthew 25:31-46).
- The kingdom is established whenever it is proclaimed and people are saved and baptized (Acts 8:12).
- The kingdom of God comes when people repent of their sins (Matthew 3:2; 4:17).
- The kingdom of God is established when you bring the peace of God to a home (Luke 10:6; Matthew 10:13).
- The kingdom of God prevails when the gates of hell are breached and the devil's powers bound (Matthew 16:18-19).

The greatest *reward* of the kingdom message is found in Matthew 24:14: "And this gospel of the kingdom will be proclaimed throughout the whole world as a testimony to all nations, and then the end will come." As far as I can tell, this is the only scripture in the entire Bible that specifically gives a criterion for Jesus' return.

The Goal of the Church

It has become common in recent years for some to disparage and even discourage the need to attend a local church. I find that extremely disturbing. I have not seen positive results in the families or individuals who have chosen to take that route. Corporate worship, fellowship, prayer, and teaching of the Word are critical to one's spiritual health.

Lone Rangers don't fare well when they choose to isolate themselves from their spiritual family. The body of Christ was meant to function corporately. We are built for relationships and need the accountability found in them. Don't be guilty of encouraging people to forsake the church.

While I cannot condone the casual approach to church attendance, I do believe that we should recognize the absolute necessity of making the church a refueling station rather than the final destination. It seems very apparent that the goal of many church leaders is often to get people into the building rather than equipping them to go out to evangelize and spread the gospel of the kingdom. I heard of one pastor who explained to his staff that their vision for the coming year was to make sure there was a "butt in every seat." I fear that might be the unstated goal of many church leaders. Jesus led differently.

As a pastor, my goal was to get the "butts" out of the seats and into the world, where the lost, disenfranchised, hurting,

> We should recognize
> the absolute
> necessity of
> making the church
> a refueling station
> rather than the final
> destination.

and diseased were. If the church is like a barn, I am concerned if all the seed remains in the barn. Barns are not built to contain seed, but to distribute it, sow it, and harvest it. Seed does no good when it remains in the barn. We must get the seed of the Word of God and the message of the kingdom out of the confines of the church building and into the soil of the world.

I always taught my congregations to minister salvation, healing, and baptism to people who are still in the world. Don't wait until they can come to church. Church attendance would explode if the members were equipped to minister to people where they are, in their jobs, offices, and public activities, rather than try to relocate them first to a building for salvation, healing, and deliverance. Our call is to take the Gospel to the world, not expect the world to come to us. Even what we call "communion" should occur first in the home before it ever reaches the church. Jesus wasn't in a synagogue or the

Temple when He served the bread and wine to the disciples, but in a home.

The GO Gospel

When I read Matthew 28:18-19, it becomes clear to me that the Great Commission is a "go" gospel, not a "come" gospel. "Come to our church, come hear our preacher, come and be part of our worship experience, come see our children's department, come and enjoy our Christmas pageant and Easter presentation, come to the altar for salvation and prayer."

I don't disparage any of these programs. I believe they are important and may be necessary. However, it still begs the question: where is the church most effective, in the small enclave of the building or out in the real world? Where are the diseased, disenfranchised, destitute, demon-possessed, and discouraged located? For the most part they are in the world, needing to hear the message of the kingdom.

From the scriptures and examples I've listed in this chapter, it appears to me that a "Go" gospel is more effective than a "Come" gospel.

- Go and heal the sick.
- Go and cast out demons.
- Go and deliver the oppressed.
- Go and raise the dead.
- Go and lead people to Jesus.
- Go and be a witness to the world of what God has done for you.
- Go and make disciples.

The Great Commission is a "go" gospel, not a "come" gospel.

- Go and tread upon the territory of Satan and proclaim Jesus as the new owner.
- Go and visit the sick and imprisoned.
- Go and preach the gospel of the kingdom.
- Go and help people lift the heavy load they carry.
- Go and invade the darkness with your light.
- Go and baptize people in the name of the Father, Son, and Holy Spirit.
- Go and freely give that which you've been given.
- Go and establish kingdom-oriented businesses.
- Go and spread the limitless love of God.
- Go and invite them to dinner.

GO! GO! GO!

When we get the "Go" Gospel down, the "Come" Gospel will be soon to follow. "Come to me, all who labor and are heavy laden, and I will give you rest" (Matthew 11:28).

But remember, you are not inviting people to a church building, to hear a sermon, participate in a program, become a member, or join a denomination. You are inviting them to Jesus, their Savior, the Head of the Church and the King of His kingdom.

Who Are the Feet of Jesus?

If the enemy is under the feet of Jesus, then we, the body of Christ, have the responsibility of destroying the works of the devil. The feet are part of the body. It is the church which has been assigned to crush the head of Satan. Romans 16:15 says, "The God of peace will soon crush Satan under your feet."

To the disciples in Luke 10:19, Jesus said, "Look, I have given you authority over all the power of the enemy, and you can walk among snakes and scorpions and crush them" (NLT). Again, it's the feet of Jesus, the body of Christ, which does the crushing.

The first prophecy of the Bible is in Genesis 3:15: "I will put enmity between you and the woman, and between your offspring and hers; he will crush your head, and you will strike his heel" (NIV).

This verse refers to Jesus the Messiah in His victory over Satan. The prophetic revelation of this finds its fulfillment at the cross and extends through the age of grace. Jesus crushed Satan's head at the cross and continues to do so through the church militant. I'm sure this is what Jesus alludes to in Matthew 16:18 when He says, "On this rock I will build my church, and the gates of hell shall not prevail against it." Even the stronghold of Satan is incapable of stopping the conquering, kingdom-minded church.

It is the responsibility of the body of Christ on this earth to destroy the devil's kingdom. If the stated reason for the appearance of Jesus on this earth was to destroy the works of the devil, then that should be the stated purpose for the church as well. "The reason the Son of God appeared was to destroy the devil's work" (1 John 3:8 NIV).

Paul makes clear in 1 Corinthians 15:24-28 that before Jesus ultimately hands the kingdom over to God the Father at His return, every rule, authority, and power will be put under His feet. Since the church is the body of Christ, to which the feet are attached, it is clear to me that the church must be integrally involved in establishing the kingdom of God on this earth by putting the kingdom of Satan under its feet. Territory that has been claimed by Satan needs to be re-claimed by the Church for Jesus.

The goal of every leader should not be to build a bigger congregation, but to see entire cities won to Christ.

If, knowing the immensity of Satan's global power and influence, this sounds like an insurmountable task, be encouraged by the words of Jesus to the seventy disciples after they returned from their kingdom campaign. While they reported to Jesus the joy of seeing demons cast out of people, Jesus revealed the larger cosmic picture, which is much more impressive. "I saw Satan fall like lightning from heaven" (Luke 10:18). Don't be discouraged, dear friend, in your daily administration of kingdom authority. As you, the body of Christ, are active ministering to people, in the unseen world Satan is being ejected from His heavenly seat of power by Jesus, the Head of the church.

Another Weapon

Don't underestimate the power of prayer in binding and defeating Satan and his minions. *When your knees bend in prayer, your feet crush the head of the enemy.*

In answer to Daniel's prayer in Daniel 9, Gabriel and the archangel, Michael, were dispatched from heaven to completely foil the devil's plans for Iran, which is ancient Persia, and Greece. Based on what we see in Daniel, it is also my belief that the binding of Satan for a thousand years, mentioned in Revelation 20, is a direct result of the prayers of the saints. Revelation 5:8 and 8:3 also make clear that it's the prayers of the saints which are used to open the seals to the end-time events.

May I remind you again, this whole topic of prayer and the kingdom started when Jesus commanded us to *pray* for God's will to be done and His kingdom to come on earth as it was in heaven. Matthew 6:10.

In Ephesians 6:17-18, after Paul lists the defensive armor we are to put on in order to deflect the enemy's assault, such as the shield of faith and the breastplate of righteousness, He then mentions two offensive weapons, the sword of the Spirit and prayer. I'm sure you've heard of weapons of mass destruction? Well, these are weapons of mass salvation.

The End of the Kingdoms of the World

First Corinthians 15:24-28 gives you the final scenario that Daniel described more than 2,500 years ago, when all the kingdoms of the world are put under the feet, or authority, of Jesus. This is one of the most powerful, climactic verses in the entire Bible: "Then comes the end, when he delivers the *kingdom* to God the Father after destroying every rule and every authority and power. For he must reign until he has put all his enemies under his feet." The grand scheme of all history is for God's kingdom to prevail over the kingdom of the devil, and the instrument God has chosen to complete the task is Jesus' body, the church.

God put people on your team, and He didn't call them for salvation only. He didn't call them to only be good church members on Sunday. He called them to destroy the demons of darkness and crush the head of the Serpent (Luke 10:19; Romans 16:20). If all we're producing is a church full of faithful attenders and givers, we've failed. Our churches should be filled with warriors armed with the Word of God and filled with the Holy Spirit. They should be elite soldiers, intent on seeing Satan's kingdom destroyed and God's kingdom established. Are you leading them into battle? Are you leading differently?

Every member must be supported and encouraged to seek God's kingdom first. Each member should be taught to use his or her gifts—in the market place, in the home, in the civic community, and in the sports fields. "Seek first the kingdom" isn't just a cute phrase—it's the heart of the gospel and the purpose of the entire Word of God.

Satan Is the Ruler of This World

The Bible clearly declares that the kingdoms of the world presently belong to Satan. These are the words of Jesus: "Now is the judgment of this world; now will the ruler of this world be cast out" (John 12:31). "I will no longer talk much with you, for the *ruler* of this world is coming. He has no claim on me" (John 14:30). Jesus again called Satan "the *ruler* of this world" in John 16:11. If on three occasions Jesus called Satan the ruler, the *archon* of this world, we can trust this is the case.

In another reference Paul identifies Satan as the "god of this world" (2 Corinthians 4:4). First John 5:19 states that the entire world is in the power of the evil one. Ephesians 2:2 describes Satan as the ruler of the authorities of the air. Revelation 9:11 reveals either Satan or one of his minions as the King of the Abyss. If that's the case, the devil has a whole lot of authority, extending from the heavens above to the Abyss below the earth.

In the wilderness temptation, the devil had the audacity to offer all the kingdoms of the world to Jesus if only He would fall down and worship him (Matthew 4:9). Rather, Jesus chose to die on the cross and through death destroy the power of the devil (Hebrews 2:14). Now Jesus has commissioned the church, His body, to put the devil's kingdom under His feet.

The Groaning of Creation

Man's sin brought mankind and all of creation into captivity. Though people are individually set free from the devil's oppression, the creation as a whole is not (Romans 8:20-22). The whole creation groans, wanting and waiting to be delivered from the dominion of the devil.

I can't imagine what it will be like when Satan, along with the other members of his demonic trilogy, the Antichrist and the False Prophet, along with all the kingdoms of the world, evil rulers, despotic leaders, haters of God, inventors of sin, all pornographers, all false religious leaders, every demon in and out of hell, and every evil person, living or dead, will bow their knees to Jesus and proclaim Him as Lord (Philippians 2:10-11).

Revelation 11:15 is one of my favorite scriptures in the entire Bible. As soon as the seventh trumpet sounds, loud voices in heaven will proclaim, "The kingdom of the world has become the kingdom of our Lord and of his Christ, and he shall reign forever and ever." This verse corresponds to Revelation 19, when Jesus returns for the second time to this earth for the purpose of destroying all the kingdoms of the world in the great battle of Armageddon (see Revelation 16:16). Let's listen to Jesus' own words on what will happen at His second coming:

> Immediately after the tribulation of those days the sun will be darkened, and the moon will not give its light, and the stars will fall from heaven, and the power of the heavens will be shaken. Then will appear in heaven the sign of the Son of Man, and then all the tribes of the earth will mourn, and they will see the Son of Man coming on the clouds of heaven with power and great glory. And he will send out his angels with a loud trumpet call, and they will gather his elect from the four winds, from one end of heaven to the other. (Matthew 24:29-31)

In December 1741, the greatest oratorio of all time, George Frideric Handel's *Messiah*, was first performed in Dublin, Ireland. In the centuries since this first performance, multiplied millions of people have risen to their feet as the choir sings the Hallelujah Chorus. Many different stories have arisen over the years about when the practice of standing for the Hallelujah Chorus actually began. Some say it was when King George II of England stood, and the audience, according to tradition, obliged and stood for the king. Whether that story is myth or history cannot be known. But I can tell you without equivocation that when Jesus returns and the kingdoms of this world have become the kingdom of our Lord and of His Christ, it will be time to break out into the heavenly Hallelujah Chorus. But instead of all standing, all will fall at the feet of Jesus and proclaim Him King of kings and Lord of lords.

Can I hear someone shout, "Hallelujah!"

One of the most powerful, prophetic verses in all the Bible is found in Daniel 7:21-22: "As I looked, this horn [meaning the Antichrist] made war with the saints and prevailed over them, until the Ancient of Days came, and judgment was given for the saints of the Most High, and the time came when the saints possessed the kingdom."

Do you ever feel worn down by the devil's tactics? Do you ever just get tired of fighting? I've got good news.

A few verses later, Daniel 7:27 says, "And the kingdom and the dominion and the greatness of the kingdoms under the whole heaven shall be given to the people of the *saints* of the Most High; his kingdom shall be an everlasting kingdom, and all dominions shall serve and obey him."

Do you really understand what that means? (You can start rejoicing any minute now.)

The devil will lose the greatest battle in all history and all the kingdoms of the world will be given to the saints and they will possess it forever. Can I hear another "Hallelujah!"

Leaders who *lead differently* will make the kingdom of God their priority.

CHAPTER **12**

Lead

with anointing

*Since the days of Pentecost, has the whole church ever put
aside every other work, and waited upon Him for ten
days, that the Spirit's power might be manifested? We
give too much attention to method and machinery and
resources, and too little to the source of power.*

Hudson Taylor

*"And you know that God anointed Jesus of Nazareth
with the Holy Spirit and with power. Then Jesus went
around doing good and healing all who were oppressed
by the devil, for God was with him."*

Acts 10:38 NLT

Can you imagine what the Last Supper conversation between Jesus and the disciples must have been like? The dinner is over, and Jesus begins to tell the disciples who will be taking His place.

"Uh, gents, may I have your attention? Put your lamb chop down and listen up. I want to inform you of something very special that's going to be happening within just a few days. I won't be around after tonight. I'll be gone. As in, gone where you can't find me. Secondly, though I'm gone I won't really be gone. Be encouraged. I'll have a replacement. You'll love Him. He's just like Me in every aspect. Well, nearly every aspect.

"I kid you not, He's exactly like Me, in every way, except you can't see Him, eat with Him, walk with Him, talk with Him, or tell stories together. Oh, and the fishing trips are over, so you can retire your boats and store your nets. He fishes, but not with boats and nets.

"I call Him Holy Spirit, or Spirit of Truth, or Comforter, or Advocate, or Helper. You're going to love Him.

"When's He coming? He'll arrive about fifty days from Saturday. Get ready. When He comes, He's going to blow you away. Literally.

"Now here's the really funny part. He's not going to walk with you. He's going to walk inside you. I know that's hard to believe, but it worked for me."

I can see their incredulous looks. "If we can't see Him, how will we know when He arrives?"

"Oh, you'll know," replied Jesus. "It's like asking how we'll know when a hurricane has come ashore."

I know I made the imagined conversation sound lighthearted, but it was very serious.

God's Moving In

No one in that small group of disciples could have possibly conceived how important Jesus' announcement was, or how powerful His replacement would be. The greatest event since the coming of Jesus was about to occur. Another member of the Godhead would be moving His headquarters from heaven to earth, from the heavenly temple into human temples, God's new dwelling place. Paul would refer to believers three times as temples of the Holy Spirit (1 Corinthians 3:16; 6:19; 2 Corinthians 6:16). For the first time in the history of the world, two members of the Godhead would now reside on earth: first Jesus, then after His departure, the Holy Spirit.

That's why Jesus could boldly proclaim, "It's better for you that I go away because if I don't go away the Holy Spirit cannot come. For me to reside inside you, rather than walk beside you, I have to send the Holy Spirit." The Holy Spirit was moving His headquarters from heaven to earth, and making the spirit of the believers His home. The event Jesus heralded could not have been a more monumental announcement.

The Secret of the Life of Jesus

Jesus knew something that most leaders don't: it wasn't enough to be *born* of the Spirit (Luke 1:35), *led* by the Spirit (Luke 4:1), or *empowered* by the Spirit (Luke 4:14); He must also be *anointed* of the Holy Spirit (Luke 4:18). The anointing was God's full vindication of Jesus' ministry through signs, wonders, and miracles. It was a visible, yet mysterious indication that God was showing up and moving in a powerful manifestation of His own presence through the human vessel of Jesus. It was visual, yet difficult to define. They could feel and sense that something was happening beyond human description or capacity. It was supernatural before anyone knew or could describe what supernatural was. It was the kiss of God. This was the Father saying, first to the disciples and then to the multitudes, "This is my Son; listen to Him." It brought awe, inspiration, admiration, and revelation.

In Old Testament days, when it was time to coronate a king, he would be smeared with oil by a prophet or priest as a symbol of God's full authority resting on him. In the New Testament, however, believers would experience something new. Rather than be anointed by a priest so they could rule as a king, they would be anointed by the Holy Spirit so they could establish God's kingdom, authority, and power on this earth.

Acts 10:38 makes it clear that Jesus was anointed of the Holy Spirit so He could destroy the works of the devil. This is also confirmed in 1 John 3:8. God's ultimate purpose in anointing not only His Son but you and all believers is to see Satan's kingdom destroyed and His kingdom established.

After spending forty days in the wilderness being tempted, Jesus returned to His hometown of Nazareth. He immediately went to the synagogue on the Sabbath day, as He was accustomed to doing. But something happened that no one was expecting. When the synagogue elders handed Him the scroll of Isaiah, He immediately unrolled it toward the end of the scroll, to a text we now refer to as Isaiah 61. He began to read: "The Spirit of the Lord is upon me, because he has *anointed* me to proclaim good news to the poor. He has sent me to proclaim liberty to the captives and recovering of sight to the blind, to set at liberty those who are oppressed, to proclaim the year of the Lord's favor" (Luke 4:18-19).

Did you catch it? *The secret of the life of Jesus was the anointing and power of the Holy Spirit.* No wonder the response from the congregants was every eye fixed on Him.

Luke 4:18 says that Jesus was anointed by the Holy Spirit. The author is not just giving a commentary on Isaiah 61. Rather, he is declaring that from that moment forward, Jesus is empowered to fulfill His calling, and that's exactly what happened. Not one miracle is recorded of Jesus before the anointing of Luke 4:18, but nonstop miracles occur after that. That leads me to the conclusion that if God is behind a ministry, He will anoint it, and if He anoints it, He will send the Holy Spirit to empower it. That leads me to the opposite conclusion as well: if God isn't behind something, you should not expect supernatural results, because there won't be any.

The Kiss of God

My friend, Jimmy Evans, president of Marriage Today, has a classic statement: "If it isn't God's baby, He won't kiss it." That says it all. If it's not God's idea, He won't send His Holy Spirit to empower or confirm it.

Even if a person has experienced observable demonstrations of the Spirit's anointing on his or her life in the past, there is no guarantee that anointing will continue if the person is not in lockstep with the Spirit's direction. Sin can block the anointing, disobedience can block the anointing, bad timing can withhold the Spirit's anointing, and lack of prayer can definitely hinder the Holy Spirit's presence. Without the

"If it isn't God's baby, He won't kiss it."

Spirit's anointing, you might as well be reading from the phone directory when you speak. It will have the same affect. Boring.

Do you have any idea how many good ideas have failed because they weren't anointed? From my own experience I can tell you—a lot. God is not obligated to kiss anything that did not originate from Him, including our good ideas. But if the idea did originate from God, He will send the Holy Spirit to authenticate, vindicate, confirm, and empower it to come to pass. We cannot have the Holy Spirit's power without God's anointing, and we cannot have God's anointing without His approval. Jesus was anointed and consequently empowered.

Notice that the Holy Spirit's anointing did not come upon Jesus when He was born, baptized, or led into the wilderness, but only after He came out of the wilderness. Jesus had already experienced much of the Holy Spirit's activity prior to His anointing. But the anointing came at the point when He finished the wilderness temptation and needed to be empowered to accomplish His ministry.

The possibility is more than likely that some of you who are going through great wilderness trials are probably being set up for the greatest anointing of your life. I have never known a great leader who didn't experience great trials. During the wilderness experiences, God will teach you who He is and who the devil is, and the only thing you'll have to stand on is the Word, so you'd better learn it well. It will outlive emotions any day.

> If the anointing
> of the Holy Spirit
> was crucial to the
> success of Jesus'
> ministry, it is also
> crucial to ours.

I've often had people ask me what the anointing is. It's actually easier to show than it is to explain. As soon as a leader gets up to speak, or a singer to sing, you immediately know if he or she is anointed. The atmosphere changes. There is either a sense that the anointing of the Holy Spirit is on them, or that they're merely exercising natural gifts.

Even newborn believers don't need instructions on how to sense the Holy Spirit's anointing on someone. They might not be able to tell you why, but they instinctively know, the same way a sheep knows the voice of the shepherd.

Equally as important, and something a leader must never forget, is the futility of ministering without the Holy Spirit as opposed to the eternal fruitfulness that is produced when you do. You need to tell yourself repeatedly, like Moses of old, "I won't go without your presence, God. I won't minister without your confirming and empowering Holy Spirit. I refuse to minister out of my own talents or abilities. My own techniques, personality, and hard work won't save or change anyone, much less myself. I must have the Holy Spirit's power and anointing on my life and leadership or it is all in vain."

I can't expect God's blessing without His Spirit any more than Jesus could. I know you already believe that; I can't imagine any leader alive who hasn't tried doing things on his own and failed.

Acts 10:38 says that God anointed Jesus of Nazareth with the Holy Spirit and power. How do we know He was anointed? He went about doing good and healing all who were oppressed of the devil, for God was with Him.

Baptism by Fire

The Book of Revelation describes the Holy Spirit as flames of fire before the throne (Revelation 4:5). In Matthew 3:11, John the Baptist prophesied that Jesus would baptize His church in the Holy Spirit and fire, and sure enough, in Acts 2:3, the Holy Spirit fire separated and landed on each of them, empowering the first church.

Fire, the power of God, was everywhere in the Book of Acts. It is a book of fire. If we're going to have a ministry that will shake the world, we must have the Holy Spirit fire as well. People aren't drawn to smoke or smoldering embers, nor are people's lives transformed by programs. As God said to Zechariah, "Not by might, nor by power, but by my Spirit, says the LORD of hosts" (Zechariah 4:6).

For those who insist that the days of Holy Spirit power are over, I would question why God would birth the church in power and rapture her powerless. I'm convinced that Joel

2 and Acts 2 didn't find their climax in the upper room; it was only the beginning.

It is absolutely critical that we contend for the Spirit's anointing on our ministry. The fire will either consume us or empower us; it's our call. But we cannot minister without it. If the anointing of the Holy Spirit was crucial to the success of Jesus' ministry, it is also crucial to ours.

I was speaking at a church in Houston, Texas when something very unusual happened. It was between the first and second services and I was spending additional time praying in the green room after the pastor left to begin the second service. Soon after the worship began, I walked into the back of the sanctuary and started walking toward the platform. I had barely stepped into the sanctuary when I stopped dead in my tracks. About a third of the way to the front I spotted what looked like a ray of light, or aura, suspended directly above one of the congregants. I just stood there for a few minutes trying to understand what was happening.

When I got to the platform, I looked back at the person who had appeared to be singled out by the Holy Spirit. This time, instead of seeing the light, I saw what appeared to be oil smeared on the head of the young man. It didn't take long to discern that this person had been singled out by the Holy Spirit to minister in a specific area of anointing.

After the service was over and most of the crowd had left, I moved to the back of the church, preparing to catch a return flight home. To my surprise, the oil-smeared young man was standing there, waiting to talk to me. I asked permission if I might prophesy over him relating to his ministry. As it turned out, he was a worship leader for a major youth ministry in the nation.

> All the flesh
> can produce is
> weakness, fear, and
> trembling, but the
> Spirit produces the
> power of God.

Since that day, Fernando Alvarez has traveled with me on numerous occasions, and has led worship for most of our conferences and events. He also leads worship and speaks for major churches throughout the nation and world.

It wasn't difficult for me to know that Fernando was anointed; all I had to do was follow the trail of oil.

Resting on the Power of God

Anointing—what an amazing word. It's the kiss of God. It's the smearing of the Holy Spirit that announces that anything can happen because God is here. It's the revelation that something powerful is going to happen. It's the awareness that God is in this place. It's the presence of God that can never be reproduced by any human power. It's the aroma of the perfume of the Holy Spirit as He passes by.

Paul described the Holy Spirit's anointing perfectly in 1 Corinthians 2:1-5: "And I, when I came to you, brothers, did not come proclaiming to you the testimony of God with lofty speech or wisdom. For I decided to know nothing among you except Jesus Christ and him crucified. And I was with you in weakness and in fear and much trembling, and my speech and my message were not in plausible words of wisdom, but in demonstration of the Spirit and of power, so that your faith might not rest in the wisdom of men but in the power of God."

All the flesh can produce is weakness, fear, and trembling, but the Spirit produces the power of God.

Liquid Love

In his autobiography, the great evangelist Charles G. Finney relates an experience that he had in the fall of 1821.

> But as I turned and was about to take a seat by the fire, I received a mighty baptism of the Holy Ghost. Without any expectation of it, without ever having the thought in my mind that there was any such thing for me, without my recollection that I had ever heard the thing mentioned by any person in the world, the Holy Ghost descended on me in a manner that seemed to go through me, body and soul. I could feel the impression, like a wave of electricity, going through and through me. Indeed, it seemed to come in waves and waves of liquid love; for I could not express it in any other way. It seemed like the very breath of God. I can recollect distinctly that it seemed to fan me, like immense wings.

No words can express the wonderful love that was shed abroad in my heart. I wept aloud with joy and love; and I do not know but I should say, I literally bellowed out the unutterable gushings of my heart. The waves came over me, and over me, one after the other, until I cried out, "I shall die if these waves continue to pass over me." I said, "Lord, I cannot bear any more"; yet I had no fear of death.

How long I continued in this state, with this baptism continuing to roll over me and go through me, I do not know. But I know it was late in the evening when a member of my choir—for I was the leader of the choir—came into the office to see me in this state of loud weeping, and said to me, "Mr. Finney, what ails you?" I could make him no answer for some time. He then said, "Are you in pain?" I gathered myself up as best I could, and replied, "No, but so happy that I cannot live."

As Kathryn Kuhlman would often say in her crusades several decades ago, "The Holy Spirit can do more in a second than I can do in a lifetime." It's a lesson we all should learn.

It is impossible to *lead differently* unless you lead in the anointing of the Holy Spirit. Can I hear an "Amen"?

CHAPTER 13

Lead
with vulnerability

All defensiveness and emotional tumult is a fear response because of your need for acceptance and ruthless control of the territory of your safe fantasy world.

Bryant McGill, aphorist

"He committed no sin, neither was deceit found in his mouth. When he was reviled, he did not revile in return; when he suffered, he did not threaten, but continued entrusting himself to him who judges justly."

1 Peter 2:22-23

Defensiveness is a trait I come by quite naturally. It was deeply imbedded in my nature by the actions and genetics of many grandfathers before me, and originating with my first grandfather, Adam. When God confronted him in the garden about his newly-acquired sin nature, his retort was, "The woman you gave me caused me to sin." Wow! Adam was thinking quickly on his feet. That's a classic. I've used it ever since.

Of course, the woman was quick to place the blame on someone else, that slippery snake, the devil, and to this day the descendants of Adam and Eve have become quite adept at shifting the blame.

One time, I was standing in line at a restaurant waiting to be seated when a waitress wheeled around quickly to clear more dishes off a table and ran smack-dab into me. She dumped her whole tray of Alaskan King crab shells all over a couple dining nearby. She burst into an explosive rant against me: "See what you made me do?" She was in a rage and edged forward as though getting in range to punch me.

I've been blamed for a lot of things, but this was a first. My only fault for this accident was standing in line waiting for a table. Rather than admit that she couldn't see me because of the size of her tray, she pivoted and took her wrath out on me. I was innocent and I was wrongly accused!

Who Are You Going to Blame This Time?

Since that time forty years ago, I've had ample opportunity to be *really* wrong on many, many occasions. I could offer excuses with the best of them. I've also had my opportunities to point an accusing and bony finger at the nearest person, barking out, "See what you made me do?"

A few years into our family-rearing season, I took my wife, Devi, and our two children, Aaron and Trina, to an A&W Root Beer drive-in. (Back then, rare was the town that didn't have an A&W Root Beer drive-in restaurant.)

The waitress hung the tray on our car window. There were chicken baskets, hamburgers, fries, and frosty root beer mugs, and I was about to dig in when I heard my daughter in the back seat say, "Dad, will you roll my window down, please, I'm hot." You can guess the tragic consequences of her request. Instead of hitting her back-seat window button, I fat-fingered the driver's window button. The tray hanging on the window tilted and fell hard. The ketchup looked like it had been painted down the side of the car. Fries and fried meat were everywhere. The car-hopping waitresses all stopped and ran over to help.

I wheeled around in the seat, just about to angrily say, "Trina, see what you made me do?"

My wife, Devi, said, "Who are you going to blame this time?" I was busted!

It's amazing how our nation and world are filled with people who aren't to blame for their actions. It's always someone else's fault. I'm just the victim.

"The reason I'm in prison is that my dad was a drug addict."

"The reason I'm on drugs is because my parents were abusive and I turned to drugs to deal with the pain."

"The reason I'm bitter is because I was left alone when I was a child."

What kind of fear has such a hold on us that we can never embrace personal responsibility?

"My marriage failed because my husband cheated on me."

"The reason I was late for work and got fired was because of the heavy traffic."

"The reason we lost the game was because we had a bad coach."

"I turned to alcohol because of my parent's divorce."

It's always someone else's fault; I'm never to blame. Oh, really? Why is it we're so reluctant to assume responsibility and so ready to shift the blame to someone else? What kind of fear has such a hold on us that we can never embrace personal responsibility?

Leaders and leadership candidates—hear me, please! You won't have optimal spiritual or emotional growth if you are a defensive person. Defensiveness hits you everywhere. It compromises career and personal relationships. My wife, Devi, is convinced that it is the number one enemy of intimacy in a marriage. I'm inclined to agree with her. Of course, she should know since she lives with me.

Handing Off Your Responsibility, Blame, or Guilt to Someone Else

Defensiveness is handing off your responsibility, blame, or guilt to someone else.

- Defensiveness says, "I already know what you're going to tell me, so I'm not interested in listening to you." The response of this person to any suggestion is automatically, "I know, I know."
- Defensiveness says, "I didn't do it. It's someone else's fault."
- Defensiveness says, "If you think I'm wrong, then you're wrong."
- Defensiveness says, "I will never assume blame or step up to responsibility."
- Defensiveness says, "I will blame others for my problem and consider myself a victim."
- Defensiveness insists on arguing so the blame can be shifted or postponed.
- Defensiveness says, "I would rather blame you than to embrace the pain of change."
- Defensiveness says, "I would rather remain unteachable than admit I'm wrong and grow."

Defensive people are *always* unteachable. Defensive people *love* to argue.

Defensive people are always unteachable.

Defensive people *prefer* to remain in a state of spiritual immaturity. They don't *grow.* If you're not growing, you're thwarting God's plan for your life.

By the way, defensive people rebuff instruction. They are sure they have already learned everything there is to learn.

My son was on a youth basketball team that never won a game. He would come home every night from practice, defeated, discouraged, and ready to quit. Every time, he would blame the loss of a game on the one girl who was on the team. It never occurred to him that he might be part of the problem. I wonder who he got his defensiveness from? It must have been his mother.

Why Are We Defensive?

- We want to look good.
- We fear people will think less of us if we admit our weaknesses or mistakes.
- It's a way to control our future.
- It's a way to avoid vulnerability.
- It's a way to avoid responsibility.

In our defensiveness, we often bring others in to help defend us. We play politics in the office and make calls and write memos to defend ourselves. Executives keep voluminous files they might use in the future to cover themselves from blame. We even hire defense attorneys to protect us.

Something more than sin happened in the Garden of Eden. That's when man and woman began playing the blame game. That's also when they began sewing fig leaves together to cover their nakedness, the stark proof of their sin.

I once brought a very talented young minister into my office. My goal was to help his presentation. He'd been showing alarming traits that were negative and destructive. I felt personally responsible for him since I had recommended him to several pastors, and none of them would invite him back. I felt that if I could bring some things to his attention, they could easily be corrected and he could see improvement.

We met and I began rolling out my concerns. "You over-speak your allotted time, by a long shot, totally ignoring the pastor's request."

"Congregations and pastors are getting a distinct impression that you are anti-church, and they're not interested in having you back."

"Some of your doctrine is questionable, but you're unwilling to listen to the concerns of others."

Because he claimed he had heard from Jesus directly, he instantly rejected any comment or direction on his doctrinal orthodoxy. He was right and all others were wrong. After all, who can argue with a person who plays the "Jesus told me" card?

His response was, "I've never been hurt so badly." In other words, "I'm a victim. I'm hurt, therefore I won't receive anything you said."

Defensiveness always shifts the blame to others. It's your fault because you hurt me.

Here's the issue: *if you don't assume responsibility, there is no way you can change anything.* You can never change someone else; you can only change yourself. If someone else is the problem, there is no hope for your future. *It's only when you personally assume responsibility that change is possible and likely.*

It seems to be human nature, doesn't it? I'm never to blame. Adam did it. Eve did it. Saul did it. Aaron did it, and people in the New Testament did it.

Spiritualizing Your Disobedience

When Saul didn't kill all the Amalekites, as instructed by Samuel, he said, "I have obeyed the voice of the LORD. I have gone on the mission on which the LORD sent me. I have brought Agag the king of Amalek, and I have devoted the Amalekites to destruction. But the people took of the spoil, sheep and oxen, the best of the things devoted to destruction, to sacrifice to the LORD your God in Gilgal" (1 Samuel 15:20-21).

In this example, Saul made the people the problem, even though his own disobedience was the problem. He claimed *they* just wanted to keep the animals alive so *they* could offer a sacrifice to God. He even tried to spiritualize his disobedience. Notice he also referred to the Lord as being the God of Samuel, "the LORD, *your* God," thereby absolving himself of any responsibility in the disobedience.

I think Aaron, the brother of Moses, had a much better excuse when he built the golden calf. Talk about stretching the truth! "When I threw the gold from these evil people into the fire, poof, out came this golden calf" (see Exodus 32). The truth was Aaron sculpted the idol himself, and then had the gall to blame the people with this outrageous story.

The New Testament has a great example of a defensive soul. In Matthew 25:24-25, the one-talent man buried his talent. When called to account, he said, "I knew that you are a hard man, harvesting where you have not sown and gathering where you have not scattered seed. So I was afraid and went out and hid your gold in the ground. See, here is what belongs to you" (NIV).

He even had the audacity to call his master a hard man, unreasonable, demanding, and insensitive. How do you like that for blame-shifting—all while his two non-defensive compatriots were out making money with their money.

The Buck Stops Here

We have a saying in America, "Pass the buck." Do you know where it originated?

Poker became very popular in America during the second half of the 19th century. Players were highly suspicious of cheating or any form of bias, and there's considerable folklore depicting gunslingers in shootouts based on accusations of dirty dealing. In order to avoid unfairness, the deal changed hands during sessions. The person who was next in line to deal would be given a marker. This was often a knife, and knives often had handles made of buck's horn—and the marker became known as a buck. When the dealer's turn was done, he "passed the buck."

President Truman had a sign on his desk that said, "The buck stops here," meaning, stop passing the knife. The knife stops here. I take full responsibility for my actions.

I think President Truman may be the first politician in recorded history willing to assume personal responsibility. Do you have any idea how refreshing it is to see a politician accept blame for something? It's a miracle similar in magnitude to the crossing of the Red Sea.

I think one of the reasons God chose to reveal Himself to Isaiah the prophet was because of his willingness to say, "It's me! I'm the sinner; I'm the culprit."

> Woe is me! For I am lost; for I am a man of unclean lips, and I dwell in the midst of a people of unclean lips; for my eyes have seen the King, the LORD of Hosts. (Isaiah 6:5)

Likewise, we find that Daniel, David, and Ezekiel were all quick to own up to their sins.

Defending Others

If you haven't noticed how defensive we are of others, especially our children, attend a little league baseball game. The very safety of coaches and umpires is on the line when a defensive dad is in the sidelines. "You idiot, can't you see he was safe on first base!" "Get some glasses!"

Not only am I adept at defending myself, I'm also good at defending others. Often I defend my children, my family, friends, and people I don't even know, not realizing that every time I defend someone from their bad behavior, I block them

"Your goal should be zero defensiveness."

from taking personal responsibility. The very thing necessary to bring a person into maturity is undone by my misplaced defensiveness for that person. We are so prone to defensiveness we're unwilling to let anyone take responsibility for his or her actions.

As soon as a boy is arrested for a crime, his parents are quick to jump to his defense. "It couldn't have been our boy." "He's a good boy, he couldn't have done that." No, he wasn't a good boy and he did do that.

Years ago, Devi and I served as associate pastors at a church in Oakland, California. After the service, we went to retrieve our little toddler daughter, Trina, from the church nursery, only to discover that my little darling girl had bitten a little boy's arm so hard the teeth marks were still visible an hour later. Evidently the boy didn't understand that when she said, "mine," he should have surrendered the toy immediately. I couldn't believe my little adorable daughter, with the beautiful curls and cute giggle, was capable of such injury. Our little darling was becoming a cannibal. My first thoughts were, "that couldn't be our little darling. That must have been someone else's child." If it weren't for the fact that the teeth marks seemed to match hers, I probably would have denied it to this day. I should ask Trina someday, "Trina, do you remember the time when you were two and you bit the little boy's hand so hard you nearly amputated it?" They probably have a wanted poster of her in the church nursery. Let's see if she's defensive.

In our culture, people are completely unwilling to admit that they are the problem. No one is willing to take responsibility, and that's a problem. We blame everyone but ourselves. And that's the problem. We are so prone to defensiveness we're unwilling to let anyone take responsibility for his or her actions, beginning with myself.

To again quote Bryant McGill, *"Your goal should be zero defensiveness."*

My sagacious wife, Devi, aptly says, *"Defensiveness is the number one enemy of intimacy."* She is absolutely right. There can be no intimacy in a marriage or any other relationship as long as defensiveness is allowed free play.

Zero Defensiveness

The most non-defensive person who ever lived was also the only sinless person who ever lived. Jesus Christ, our Great High Priest, never defended Himself.

"As a sheep before its shearers is silent, so He opened not His mouth" (Isaiah 53:7 NKJV).

First Peter 2:22-23 says, "He committed no sin, neither was deceit found in his mouth. When he was reviled, he did not revile in return; when he suffered, he did not threaten, but continued entrusting himself to him who judges justly."

Another telltale sign of defensiveness is arguing, yet Jesus didn't do that either (Matthew 12:19). He never cried out, He never argued, He never lifted His voice.

My friend Joe told me of a corporate meeting he was recently in that perfectly exposed the defensive nature of people:

> I was in a project meeting for the financial planning platform that we rolled out last year. As the meeting progressed, we slowly felt a cold horror. We realized the product was going to roll-out incomplete and missing a key feature.
>
> The room grew quiet. I could see from the body language that everyone was rapidly shifting into a blaming mode and defensive posture to protect themselves from blame.
>
> I said to the room, "Okay, I can see from everyone's expression that we're now completely focused on who's to blame. Would it be helpful if I just took the blame right now?" (It was my project and regardless of whose specific fault it was, I own the project so in the end it's mine anyway.)
>
> The looks across the room were mixed—some were relieved and others were trying to figure out what the catch was, so I said, "Look—while we try to figure out who is to blame, we aren't focusing on the problem, let alone solving it, and even if we were all to agree who is to blame, it won't change what we have to do and that is to fix this thing. For that to happen, I need everyone focused, so let's just agree that it's my fault and move on."
>
> It took about two more minutes of discussion and then we moved on to fixing the issue. What's funny about all of it is that no one really got mad about it and because we didn't argue about it, it only came up one more time (with my

boss), and he said the same thing—as long as it gets fixed, I'm good with it.

That is a perfect example of someone who emulated the spirit of Jesus. *Jesus assumed all the blame and took it to the cross.*

In the Old Testament, a special day was chosen, the Day of Atonement. On this day, all the sins Israel committed the previous year were to be atoned for. But the unusual thing was, rather than one animal to be chosen as a sin offering, two were chosen. One of the goats, however, was not sacrificed but released into the wilderness, to wander forever until it died of natural causes. The released goat was called *Azazel,* or the scapegoat.

The Bible says that not only did Jesus cleanse your sins, but He removed them, like the scapegoat, as far as the east is from the west (Psalm 103:12). *The only sinless person who ever lived took all your excuses, justifications, defenses, and blame-shifting and forever removed them. You never need to be defensive again.* Is there an Amen in the house?

Who Is Your Defender?

I responded to a slightly deranged neighbor of mine (I'm trying to be nice by saying "slightly") who accused me of blowing my tree leaves into her yard. Standing there in the yard, I told her, "I didn't blow leaves into your yard. You blew the leaves into my yard."

Of course, she responded with an equally mature, "You liar, you did it."

"No, I didn't."

"Yes, you did, and you're a liar." Then she added the coup d'état, "And you're a preacher."

"Yes, I'm a preacher and preachers don't lie." Well, that was a lie. Preachers lie all the time. Talk about insulted!

How would you respond to a slightly deranged neighbor falsely accusing you of lying? I responded the only way my defensive nature knew how: "No, I'm not, you're the liar." Why didn't I shut up the moment she accused me? I think it's because I have more of a goat nature than a sheep nature. Why couldn't I have assumed responsibility and said, "I'm so sorry; I'll try to see that it never happens again." What is it about my human nature that wants to run from any form of accusation? Why can't I assume responsibility and carry the blame myself?

Another friend of mine, Ron Campbell, a prophet in the Dallas area, had a great suggestion. "If you could meet the person responsible for all your problems and kick them in the pants, you would not be able to sit for a week!" I read his quote on Facebook, immediately followed by a defensive person's post telling him why he was wrong, thereby proving his point.

I'm still blown away by Isaiah's response to seeing the vision of the Lord in Isaiah 6, "It's me, Lord." That's the attitude I want at all times.

Jesus, Your Defense Attorney

Jesus stood before His accusers and refused to defend Himself. If the only person who never sinned could stand silently under attack, then surely we can.

If you're wrong, you don't need to defend yourself; you're wrong.

If you're right, you don't need to defend yourself; you're right.

Jesus is our defense and the Holy Spirit is our defense, therefore you never need to defend yourself. When you stand before Jesus on Judgment Day, you will not be able to say one word in your own defense.

Jesus is your defense attorney before the Father and the Holy Spirit is your defense attorney before Jesus. There is no need to defend yourself. If Jesus and the Holy Spirit aren't good enough to represent you, you stand little chance of succeeding by defending yourself.

Many years ago, I brought my entire church leadership staff together for our monthly meeting. Wishing to appear totally open and vulnerable, I asked the group, "Is there anyone here who has anything to share concerning my leadership style?" I was sure that one or two would have something to share that would improve my leadership. I didn't think that all twenty would.

Most of the suggestions were either trivial or lacked helpful specifics. One, however, was ruthless in his comments. My administrator brought heavy artillery and left me shell-shocked.

"You don't listen to anyone. You're totally defensive. If we try to correct you, you turn it back on us. You're totally unteachable." He didn't spare anything, including my fragile emotions.

By the time he got through, I was devastated. I didn't sleep at all that night.

The next day I was scheduled to speak at a conference at Messiah College, just a few miles from where I was pastor. I pulled myself out of bed, tired from lack of sleep, eyes puffy from spending hours crying, and emotionally exhausted from the vicious attack. I got in the car and headed to Messiah College, with full intentions of asking the conference chairman if I could be excused from my commitment. But the strangest thing happened as I drove to the campus.

Instead of heading to the college, it was like an unseen hand pulled my car to the exit that led to my church and office parking lot. Within the few seconds that elapsed between when I left the highway and the four right turns required to turn into the parking lot, I heard the unmistakable voice of my Lord. "Larry, I've tried to use your enemies to tell you you're defensive. I've tried to use your friends to tell you you're defensive. I've tried to use your wife to tell you you're defensive. Now I'm using your administrator to tell you you're defensive. If you do not listen and deal with your defensiveness, I will remove your anointing."

I knew exactly what He was talking about. I didn't feel He was talking about my salvation, but my effectiveness in ministry. I could never come into full maturity as long as I was defensive. My defensive nature would eventually cost me my anointing. I knew God was serious.

I pulled into the parking lot and proceeded directly into the administrator's office. I thanked him for rebuking me, calling me out on my defensiveness, and even risking his job by confronting me. Talk about liberated. It felt like chains were falling off me.

I proceeded to the conference, but rather than excuse myself, I stood up and began to prophesy alongside the South African speaker. I have never done that in my entire life! I have no doubt the degree of anointing was commensurate with the degree of repentance for my life-long defensiveness.

Bryant McGill says, "You can get to a place where you see clearly; that place is zero defensiveness." That's the place I want to be. What about you? Good leaders don't defend themselves.

CHAPTER 14

Lead
with compassion

*Too often we underestimate the power of
a touch, a smile, a kind word, a listening
ear, an honest compliment, or the smallest
act of caring, all of which have the
potential to turn a life around.*

Leo Buscaglia

*"When he saw the crowds, he had compassion for them,
because they were harassed and helpless, like sheep
without a shepherd."*

Matthew 9:36

As a student of the Word, I've always been fascinated by the nearly hidden gems found in scripture. You might miss them in a casual reading, but if you look for them, they are there for the taking. For instance, for years I've been curious as to why Jesus rarely called Himself the Son of God. Others called Him the Son of God, but Jesus did not, preferring rather to refer to Himself as the Son of Man. In modern translations of the Bible, the "Son of Man" is capitalized. I'm not sure Jesus would even have done that.

- The devil said to Jesus, "If you are the Son of God" (Matthew 4:3).
- Demons called Him "Son of the Most High God" (Luke 8:28).
- The angel Gabriel called Jesus the Son of the Most High (Luke 1:32).
- The disciples called Jesus the Son of God (Matthew 14:33).
- Peter called Jesus, "the Christ, the Son of the living God" (Matthew 16:16).
- The centurion called Jesus the Son of God (Mark 15:39).
- God called Jesus His Son (Mark 1:11).
- Mark called Jesus the Son of God (Mark 1:1).
- Unclean spirits called Jesus the Son of God (Mark 3:11).
- Nathaniel called Jesus the Son of God (John 1:49).
- John the Baptist called Jesus the Son of God (John 1:34).

Why did so many people call Jesus the Son of God, yet He rarely referred to Himself in that way? It appears that virtually everyone called Jesus the Son of God except Jesus! Jesus calls Himself "the Son" in John 3:35, 36; 5:19, 20, 21, 22, 23, 26, but only on three occasions did He call Himself the Son of God (John 5:25; 10:36; 11:4).

By comparison, Jesus calls Himself the "Son of Man" 83 times in the Gospels.

Caiaphas tried to get Jesus to admit His true identity: "'I adjure you by the living God, tell us if you are the Christ, the Son of God.' Jesus said to him, 'You have said so. But I tell you, from now on you will see the *Son of Man* seated at the right hand of Power and coming on the clouds of heaven'" (Matthew 26:63-64, emphasis added).

Notice how Jesus turns the question back on Caiaphas, but with a response that affirms His earlier declarations: "From now on you will see the *Son of Man*." Did Jesus not know He was the Son of God? Of course He did! On several occasions, Jesus openly states that He is the Son of God. Why then does He refer to Himself the great majority of times as the Son of Man?

It seems that when you're the Son of God, you're not given to talking about it. Instead, miracles prove it, the Father proves it, all the disciples prove it, and demons, to their eternal shame, admit it. But the breathtaking truth is that when you're the Son of Man, you have no choice but to bleed, to cry, to touch, to hurt, to sympathize, and to show compassion. It's more than what you do; it's who you are, and it emanates from your very being.

Jesus calls Himself the "Son of Man" 83 times in the Gospels.

Compassion: To Suffer with Someone

I don't find it necessary to go around telling everyone that I'm a Christian. I would rather demonstrate the heart of Jesus, a heart of compassion. Nothing shows the character of Jesus more than His compassion for the hurting, diseased, despised, rejected, marginalized, and unclean of society. When mankind sees the acts of Jesus, when they see His profoundly compassionate miracles, what is mankind to conclude?

The word *compassion* literally means to suffer with someone. As Paul said, when one member of the body suffers, we all suffer (1 Corinthians 12:26). Isaiah 53:4 says, "Surely he has borne our griefs and carried our sorrows." The same scripture, quoted in Matthew 8:17, says, "He took our illnesses and bore our diseases."

Jesus didn't come to this world to show us how big and powerful God was. He came to reveal the love and compassion of the Father. He was the *Son of God*, but He came to reveal Himself as the *Son of Man*. He came to show how much the Father loves the hurting, diseased, depressed, and despised.

He came to cry and suffer with us, not to rebuke us for crying.

Now hear this! We have the same mandate as Jesus. Though we too are *sons of God* through our new birth and

> # He came to cry and
> # suffer with us, not to
> # rebuke us for crying.

baptism into Jesus Christ, *our calling is not to call attention to our identity, but to reveal our compassion.* We have an obligation to become *sons of man* so people can see the Son of God in all His compassionate glory. If we don't reveal God's love through our compassion, people will never see God.

The Greek word for compassion actually comes from the root word meaning "spleen." The ancients considered the spleen to be the most sensitive visceral organ, deep within our bodies. This spleen-like compassion emanates from the deepest part of our emotions. Literally, when someone else hurts, we embrace their pain.

The Compassion of Christ

Consider the depth of compassion carried by Jesus:

- He allowed lepers to touch Him, thus making Him unclean.
- He permitted a woman with a blood condition to touch His garment, also making Him unclean.
- He touched the multitudes with His hands, certainly posing the threat of contamination.
- He held the children in His arms and blessed them.

- He delighted in being in the presence of sinners.
- He revealed Himself to the outcasts of society.
- He had compassion on the shepherd-less multitudes.
- He cried at the tomb of Lazarus.
- He cried over Jerusalem.
- He had compassion on the bereaved mother.
- He had compassion on the crowds who had followed Him for three days without food.
- He saved an adulterous woman from certain death by stoning.

As you can see, Jesus took on the infirmities, sicknesses, sins, and concerns of the people, something modern clergy would probably find disdainful and annoying. Was Jesus passing judgment on these people? No! *The very heart and intention of Jesus was compassion.* It burst forth in miracles, words, and actions. His compassion moved hearts and healed bodies. No, Jesus came not to judge, but to heal and restore. In these powerful acts of love and healing, there was no room for judgment.

A pastor friend and his wife were visiting a large church and during the service all visitors were invited to the reception room if they wanted to meet one of the pastors. While her husband checked on another part of the church's program, his wife excitedly made her way to the reception hall. She wanted to learn how a mega-church made folks feel welcome. Yet, to her horror and dismay, she saw the pastor immediately wash his hands with hand sanitizer after meeting each guest. Still, she extended her hand to him. He paused before shaking her hand. He was still sanitizing from the last person he'd met.

Imagine Jesus doing that. It's hard to imagine, isn't it? Jesus took on the diseases and weaknesses and deep wounds of those He touched. He drew it all to Himself, willingly. Such a pastor should never go to the poor and ailing in other countries. Nor should the fear in the pastor, the fear of taking on the ailments and parasites and problems of the sick and broken, be shown to the suffering. Imagine Jesus using hand sanitizer.

Has Your Heart Grown Calloused?

Do you know why large ministries sometimes fail? I'll tell you. The leader of a failing ministry has disconnected from his flock. He no longer hurts when they hurt, nor does he bleed when they bleed. He no longer aches when they ache or cry when they cry. No longer does he stop everything he's doing to draw near to someone suffering or to stand with someone under the stifling weight of depression. In a sense, he's become emotionally jaundiced and maybe cynical.

Jesus knew that the loving embrace of the Son of Man would do more to cure humanity than the sterilized perfectionism of the Pharisees. Jesus didn't fear being polluted by an unclean world. In fact, the Son of Man came to live among us in this unclean world and to seek and save the lost (Luke 19:10). We must never forget that the lost are dirty people.

I fear church leaders are losing their compassion for the lost. We're so busy being religious "sons of God," we have no time to be "sons of man." On September 21, 2016, a refugee boat off the coast of Egypt capsized, with only 150 out of 600 people saved. Does that bother you? Does the picture of the little boy washed up on the beach in Turkey bother you, or maybe the picture of the dad crying for his two sons? Can you remember the video of the little Syrian boy wiping blood from his forehead when they placed him in the ambulance? His brother had already been killed. How did you respond? Imagine how Jesus would respond.

Eleven million refugees have fled Syria since the conflict began in 2011. Does anyone pray? Does anyone cry? Does anyone do anything? Are there any "sons of man" in the crowd? Who decides to pull alongside the trudging refugee and walk with him? We must understand; *we must burn this into our consciousness: we have been called to trudge along with the refugee.*

Over 470,000 have already been killed in the Syrian conflict. I feel pain in my innermost being. I can't read it without praying, crying, and asking God, *What can I do?*

While I'm not for illegal immigration, I am for immigration. How can I not be? I was a stranger and He took me in. I was naked and He clothed me. I was lost and He found me. I was blind when He gave me sight. *I was in prison and He visited me.* These deprivations are mentioned by Jesus in Matthew 25. They are descriptions of all of us at one time or another. Should we not in turn be the ones who clothe, visit, feed, and weep over the circumstances of hurting people? Do this and you will find the joy of your salvation.

Are we afraid of being contaminated by the sin and filth of the world? Are we afraid of catching something that could kill us?

Are we afraid of losing our reputation or being identified with grubby people?

Are we afraid of disrupting our comfortable lifestyle or being associated with sinners?

Weeping with Those Who Weep

I was in Brazil when I heard that Daniel, the son of Pastor David and Donna Diaz from Baldwin Park, California, had just been murdered. Daniel, the youth pastor at New Beginnings Church in West Covina, was taking youth home from a church outing when a young man on the sidewalk pumped three bullets into his chest. The murderer said he was seeking revenge for the killing of his friend by a Hispanic man, so he randomly chose Daniel, a complete stranger.

Devi, our assistant Felipe, and I were in the airport getting ready to board a plane to Palmas, Brazil when we got the news of Daniel's killing. We cried so hard and deeply that everyone in the airport became quiet and stared at us. I immediately flew to California from Brazil so I could weep with the family. I don't know if I did any good, but I had to be there. That's all I knew to do. I drew alongside and suffered with them. I did what I thought Jesus would do; He's my role model. Jesus would weep with the family.

Every day there are small acts of cruelty as well as mammoth crimes against humanity. Jesus' examples of compassion light a path and show us where to go and what to do. When people hurt, we must hurt with them. When they cry, we need to mingle our tears with theirs. When people are bound, we need to loosen their restraints; when imprisoned, we need to be there visiting them. Don't be deceived; there is nothing more authentic than your personal appearance at the places where the sick and the broken suffer. Be there.

Years ago, I discovered that a prison inmate's family in Philadelphia was being horribly taken advantage of. The wife owned a small neighborhood grocery store. She was robbed almost daily, and the woman could do nothing about it. Thugs constantly stole and threatened her life. She was living a nightmare.

I rented a truck and drove to Philadelphia. I loaded up the wife and her family and brought them back to our home. We lived three hours away from her store. We rented an apartment, furnished it, bought the groceries, and paid the rent until her husband was released from prison. What I'm trying to show is that compassion doesn't merely say "I love you"; compassion compels us to respond until there is relief for the oppressed. Compassion engages us to work, to heal, to appear in person, and *not quit* until we see relief.

In Luke 10, Jesus tells the story of a man walking from Jerusalem to Jericho who was beaten by thieves and left for dead. When the priest and a Levite were the first ones to see the bloodied victim, they moved to the other side of the road to avoid him. The despised Samaritan traveler, however, stopped and offered healing, relief, and future provision to the man.

Which option would Jesus have chosen and which option should you choose, following the powerful compassionate motivations of Jesus?

Act as Jesus Would Act

The Samaritan who had compassion on the fallen traveler was judged by Jesus as greater than all the passersby even though they were highly religious. *Do not play the religious card, the "Son of God" card, when someone lies bleeding and broken, when the need for compassion arises. Be the son of man. Do not* run to your closet and pray in this moment of emergency. Bind the wounds with bandages; reassure the person with the troubled and unclear mind. Bind the demonic and help lift the wounded into the ambulance. Be there in your actions.

I saw a picture of a boy on the streets of one of our cities, lying without warm clothes or covering. He was freezing on the street as people walked by, staring at the shivering boy but doing nothing to warm him. No one offered a blanket or help. People walking by must have thought, "What can I do? There is suffering everywhere." That may be true, but the shivering wide-eyed boy is right in front of *you* now, and in that moment, you must act as Jesus would act.

Several years ago, a pastor in Sarasota, Florida decided to demonstrate to his church what compassion looks like. He did not put on his Sunday suit. He clothed himself in the dirty, ragged clothes of a street person. Rather than mount the steps to the podium, he laid down in the gutter near the church parking lot entrance.

Hundreds of cars drove past this destitute, disgusting, seemingly intoxicated man in the gutter so they could enter the church in their Sunday finery to worship God. When it was time for the pastor to preach, he didn't show up. Instead, a disgusting, dirty man from the gutter walked up to the pulpit. To their horror, the pastor revealed himself as the man in the gutter. It was easier for them to worship God than to make themselves dirty by pulling someone out of the filthy gutter.

We can often make our own self-righteous judgments. Have you said, "Why doesn't he work? I have to work for a living." "He's probably on drugs." "Where are his parents?" "It's not my problem he's a drunk; he needs to will himself back to sobriety." These statements stop the flow of God's compassion through you. Think about it. Are we hiding behind petty rationalizations when we make such judgments? Sure we are, or else we would push the crowd of onlookers aside and act like Jesus.

Are You a Son of Man or a Son of God?

Years ago, I went through the deepest trial of my life. In 1980, I lost everything—my ministry, my home, my car, my income, my friends, and my reputation, and I nearly lost my mind in the process. One of the most painful losses was my confidence to preach the Gospel or even hear from God.

One of my closest friends stole over two million dollars from our ministry, effectively destroying in a matter of months what it took me twelve years to build. I can't tell you the depth of depression. Actually, I can. For over four years I remained in deep depression and even contemplated suicide.

During those days, I heard the Lord speak to me. He did not speak to me immediately, nor did I hear Him in close intervals. But very clearly, I heard the unmistakable voice of the Lord on several occasions. It's amazing how much clearer and sensitive our hearing is when we're flat on our backs. The prone position evidently improves the auditory receptors.

On one of those occasions, when I was quiet before the Lord, I heard Him speak to me: "Larry, you no longer cried. You no longer felt moved by the infirm and suffering. You had become professional. I could no longer speak through you because you became insensitive to the needs of the people. You would give them spiritually appropriate words, but you didn't hurt, or cry, or touch them, or bind up their wounds, or bear their sorrows." I felt like the Levite who saw the bloodied Jericho victim and passed by on the other side of the street.

I came to realize that God had to break me. I had become so concerned about church growth that my heart had hardened and become stone. I was more concerned about our rapidly-growing numbers and administrative demands and I became distracted. I forgot to follow my natural first inclinations as a pastor and lost touch with the suffering and challenges of the sheep. I was like an unbroken alabaster box. The most fragrant and expensive perfume was trapped inside me. My heart was hardening and the perfume couldn't flow out and be used to wash the feet of the suffering.

I had lost my heart as a son of man. *Unknowingly I had become a son of God—religious but not real.*

Several months later, Devi and I were invited to a pastor's conference in California. At one of the sessions where only the conference leaders were present, a friend of mine and prophet of God, Campbell McAlpine, shared with the leaders what I had been through. One of the guest speakers, Jack Hayford, came over to me, and without saying a word, he knelt and began to cry over my feet. With his head buried in my feet he sobbed. I sobbed. Everyone in the room sobbed. Though everyone there were godly men, *sons of God* if you will, at that moment they looked like Jesus, *sons of man.*

Many years ago, a pastor friend of mine, Jerry Cook, from Gresham, Oregon, was approached by a man in his congregation following the Sunday morning service. "Pastor, I've heard you had open heart surgery. Do you mind if I trace the scars on your chest?" Jerry thought it was an unusual request, but he shyly unbuttoned his shirt. The man said, "Pastor, I'm having

> ## Unknowingly I had become a son of God—religious but not real.

open heart surgery tomorrow. I thought it might help lessen my fears if I could touch your scars." The man began tracing the scars with his fingers.

That's what Jesus did in the Upper Room for Thomas. "Thomas, you can touch my scars. You can put your fingers on the nail prints; you can trace the scars where the spear pierced my side. I'm touchable." How would Thomas know how to relate to people if His Master refused to let Himself be touched? I pray to God we never become so professional that people can no longer touch our scars. And we should always touch theirs.

I pray we never become so successful that we don't cry when people hurt. I pray we will always be "sons of man." We've already been made sons of God by Jesus' death and resurrection. We don't need to work on that. It's a gift. But compassion is not. It must be practiced on a daily basis. Real leaders step forward, out of the crowd, and weep for the broken and the needy. They move ahead into imitating Jesus' acts of compassion. The result is that the heart of Jesus is made visible to all. He is amongst us once again.

Real leaders *lead differently*; they know how to cry.

CHAPTER 15

Lead

with faithfulness

Your faithfulness makes you trustworthy to God.

Edwin Louis Cole

"Well done, good and faithful servant. You have been faithful over a little; I will set you over much. Enter into the joy of your master."

Matthew 25:21

Have you ever heard of Rosie Ruiz? No? Well, I'm not shocked!

On April 21, 1980, Rosie won the Boston Marathon's female category with a time of 2:31:56, the fastest ever for a woman. This was also the third-fastest time recorded by any woman in any marathon.

It was an unbelievably fast time. If my math is good, that's running 26.2 miles at an average of just under six minutes per mile.

But as the ink was drying on the sports pages, it soon became apparent—it really *was* unbelievable. Not long after the race, suspicions and nagging questions surfaced. Why was Rosie not sweating? Why didn't Rosie look fatigued? And why did Rosie not have the look of a marathon runner, with those classic trim thighs and legs? And Rosie's resting heart rate ticked away at 76, while the resting pulse of a female runner was usually in the 50s.

Why didn't any of the leading runners notice Rosie on the course?

And what about the New York Marathon, held six months earlier? A reporter rode with Rosie on the subway from the beginning of the marathon to within a half-mile of the finish line. From there, Rosie stepped onto the course, claiming she'd been injured but would now continue.

Poor Rosie. Investigators discovered she hadn't run at all. She had burst through the crowd and onto Boston's Commonwealth Avenue to become the fastest female runner ever, only to be stripped of the title. Poor Rosie. Evidently no one ever told her that it's those who start *and* finish the race who receive the reward.

We Serve a Faithful God

Here's a marvelously powerful and simple truth—kingdom people are recognized and rewarded, not for their talent, but for their faithfulness.

The Bible is filled with people who finished the race and won the crown because of their faithfulness. Conversely, the scriptures also record the lamentable stories of those whose lives ended without earning their crown through a lack of faithful endurance. Demas was such a person. "Demas, in love with this present world, has deserted me and gone to Thessalonica" (2 Timothy 4:10). *Faithfulness is a character issue, and God rewards character, not talent.*

- Moses was promoted as leader of Israel because of his faithfulness (Numbers 12:7).
- David rose to be king because he was deemed faithful as a shepherd (1 Samuel 22:14).
- Daniel was thrust into national prominence because he proved himself faithful as a slave and a prisoner of war (Daniel 6:4).
- Paul was appointed an apostle to the Gentiles because he was judged faithful by his Lord, Christ Jesus (1 Timothy 1:12).
- Believers who are proven faithful are promised the crown of life (Revelation 2:10).
- Most importantly, Jesus was exalted to the right hand of the Father because of His faithfulness:
  o "Jesus Christ, the faithful witness, the firstborn of the dead, and the ruler of kings on earth" (Revelation 1:5).

> # Kingdom people are recognized and rewarded, not for their talent, but for their faithfulness.

- o "But Christ is faithful over God's house as a son" (Hebrews 3:6).
- o "And to the angel of the church in Laodicea write: The words of the Amen, the faithful and true witness, the beginning of God's creation" (Revelation 3:14).
- o Though it doesn't use the word "faithful," the text is plain, "Jesus Christ is the same yesterday and today and forever" (Hebrews 13:8).

The most powerful promotion in the world will be at the return of Christ: "Then I saw heaven opened, and behold, a white horse! The one sitting on it is called Faithful and True, and in righteousness he judges and makes war" (Revelation 19:11). Faithfulness, in this verse, is no longer a description of greatness, but a title of majesty.

Faithfulness has its rewards. In fact, that is the *only* thing that God rewards.

I wonder who Jesus got His "faithful" trait from? Like Father, like Son.

Faithfulness is the essence of who God is.

- Paul says it in this way: "If we are faithless, he remains faithful—for he cannot deny himself" (2 Timothy 2:13).
- Deuteronomy 7:9 says, "The LORD your God is God, the faithful God."
- Isaiah 49:7 says, "Because of the LORD, who is faithful."
- First Corinthians 10:13 says, "God is faithful, and he will not let you be tempted beyond your ability."

Two of my favorite verses are in Lamentations 3:22-23, where the prophet Jeremiah declares, "The steadfast love of the LORD never ceases; his mercies never come to an end; they are new every morning; great is your faithfulness." Some scholars say that Jeremiah penned these words while being held as a prisoner in a pit in Egypt. Jeremiah was so sure of God's faithfulness and steadfastness that he proclaimed it while tethered in chains. Is there a greater testimony to God's faithfulness than Jeremiah's faith?

The only place in the Old Testament where the word "faith" is found is in Habakkuk 2:4, where *emuna* is *mistranslated* as "faith." *Emuna* should be translated as "faithful." It means steadfastness, trustworthiness, reliability, steadiness, honesty, truthfulness, and conscientiousness. *It means to keep your word.* I can't think of a better description for God than "faithful;" He keeps His word. Matthew 24:35 says, "Heaven and earth will pass away, but my words will not pass away."

Years ago, we would hear an oft-repeated, spiritually-oriented phrase bantered about. It sounded pretty righteous at first, until you thought about it: "If God said it, I believe it, and that settles it." A better and simpler version of this phrase would be, "If God said it, that settles it, no matter what I believe about it." (These little nuances are so important!)

You can count on God keeping His word.

The Measure of Your Character

At one time I asked people to define "character." As you can guess, I got a lot of responses. The one I liked was from a successful Christian businessman in Los Angeles who said, "*Character is keeping your word.*" As I pondered this definition, I decided to choose this one above the others. The bottom line of character is keeping your word. If you can't keep your word, you plainly and simply don't possess godly character.

You demonstrate your character *by what you do.* This is absolutely important and bears repeating. Your character is seen in your actions and how you attend to the smallest of details.

You do what you say you'll do.

You show up when you say you'll show up.

When you make promises, you keep them.

When you tell your wife and kids you'll be home at a certain time, you show up at or before that time. (In fact, you have no better way to coach your kids into a life of godly character.)

When you promise your family you'll take them on a vacation, you take them.

When you borrow a tool and promise to return it at a certain time, you keep your word.

When you set a deadline, you keep it.

If a true emergency arises, and you're unable to fulfill an obligation, you should contact the person as soon as possible and let them know of the delay or cancellation. If you seem to have too many emergencies and can't keep your word, well, that sounds like a character problem.

A while back, Devi and our assistant, Felipe Hasegawa, were waiting for me to arrive at a restaurant in the Dallas area so they could have lunch with me. While they waited, Felipe decided to give me a call. As he was dialing, he asked Devi, "What did people do before they had cell phones?" An older lady sitting nearby instantly replied before Devi could even respond. "We kept our word." So there you have it. Before the days of cell phones, you kept your word.

Here's another supremely important but practical thing about character. *If you promise something and later find out it's inconvenient to keep the promise, you keep your word anyway.* That's character. Though this is only one aspect of faithfulness, it's a major one. If you break this one simple, foundational rule of character, you've blown it big and the roof caves in.

Faithfulness relates to everything in life.

You made a vow to remain faithful to your wife. You keep it.

You committed your life to the lordship of Jesus Christ; you keep this promise.

If you signed up to teach a class, coach a team, tackle a project, or volunteer your time, you follow through with your commitment. Your character depends on it and God's favor requires it. If you're not faithful in the small things, God won't trust you with the big things.

If you make too many commitments and there's too much on your plate, I would counsel you to honor the promises you've already made. Then, rethink how many projects you can reasonably complete with the time you have.

Commitment means follow-through. As Nike says, "Just Do It."

No excuses. You are a person of your word because God, your Father, keeps His word.

Other Aspects of Faithfulness

Here are three key tenets of faithfulness:

- **Stability.** You're consistent. You're not up one day and down the other. You're not changing your mind all the time. You're balanced, predictable, and stable.
- **Trustworthiness.** You can be counted on. You've got your act together and you'll responsibly oversee commitments. You'll act with diligence and integrity.
- **Loyalty.** I've never met a disloyal person who was not unfaithful in many aspects of life.

When the Master Is Away

Several years ago, Devi and I took a family vacation. We left the oversight of our home to two college students who were living with us at the time. The vacation was over, and we arrived back at the house to find the front door standing wide open. Peering through the windshield of the car I was thinking, "This isn't looking good."

> # We live in God's house. As guests in this home, we're stewards on a daily basis.

Recently-fallen snow was blowing in through the open door. Quickening my pace, I went through the door, surprised to see three neighborhood dogs snoozing comfortably on our velvet sofas. I scooted them out the front door, galled by their offended looks. They obviously saw me as a cold-hearted human, herding them out into the bitter cold of winter.

It turned out that while we were gone, blissfully unaware on our holiday, the two college students threw a party for all their relatives. It wasn't a bad party, but it was a party nonetheless. They had used our finest china to prepare a meal fit for a king. The only problem was they never asked the king of the house if they could do it.

This is what Jesus was alluding to in several of His parables. *The master of the house is going on a journey, and He's leaving you with the responsibility of the house.* This is where you should bear down with all your heart and soul. How you responsibly treat the upkeep, care, and oversight of the servants and the home will determine your reward at His return.

In Hebrews 3, the Bible says that Moses was faithful in all God's house, as Jesus was in His. It's a stewardship issue, and the house, regardless of to whom it belongs, really belongs to God.

A friend of mine was asked to take care of a saltwater aquarium located at the home of some mutual friends. This gorgeous living room aquarium held thousands of dollars' worth of sea creatures, beautiful fish, crustaceans, and coral. Yes, you know what happened. The couple returned home. They did a quick status check of the aquarium. Not a fin moved. Most of the fish were floating belly-up. The aquarium had become a pet cemetery. Every single fish was dead. A post-mortem diagnosis of the situation revealed that a fish had died and hadn't been removed. The steward wasn't very stewardly. My uneducated guess is that a dead fish should be removed so the others won't die. Thousands of dollars were flushed down the drain (literally) through the lack of attentive stewardship.

Hopefully there are more stories about good and responsible stewardship than there are about botched stewardship. Faithful stewardship really is an issue of the heart.

We live in God's house. As guests in this home, we're stewards on a daily basis.

Are You a Faithful Steward?

To me one of the greatest sins against God's creation is how we've trashed it up. I can't bear to throw down a candy wrapper or a soda can. In Romans 8:21-23, Paul says the whole universe is groaning, waiting to be released from the sins we have put it under. If creation is also our responsibility, we have an obligation to maintain its pristine order in every possible way. This is not merely an ecologically sound idea; it's God's idea.

If we keep our car looking like a dumpster, our home and yard unmaintained, and our belongings strewn about, we set the pattern for poor stewardship in every area of our lives. We also pass down a horrible example to our children.

Jesus said, "One who is faithful in a very little is also faithful in much, and one who is dishonest in a very little is also dishonest in much. . . . if you have not been faithful in that which is another's, who will give you that which is your own?" (Luke 16:10, 12). It's interesting that Jesus equated sloppy stewardship with unfaithfulness.

I recently went into a Sam's Club in our area. While pushing my cart down one of the aisles, I overheard one of the managers talking with an employee. He was pointing out an empty bag of grapes in the produce department. The manager said, "People will take a bag of grapes from the display counter, eat them while they're shopping, then return the empty bag here."

I can guarantee that those people are also thieves away from the grocery store. Grapes aren't the only things they're stealing. You can bet they're poor stewards in other areas of their lives as well. My greatest concern is what they are teaching their kids. I can nearly hear them tell the judge, "I trained them well, I just don't know how they went wrong." It's a great mystery, isn't it?

While speaking one day at Christ for the Nations in Dallas, one of our favorite Bible training institutes, my wife Devi said to the students, "What makes you think that if you can't keep your room clean, your bed made, and the trash picked up, that God will entrust a ministry to you? How can you preach to thousands when you can't even pick up the litter in your own car? How can you reach the world when you don't even clean your own toilet or wash the dishes in your sink, leaving them to pile up?"

As I roamed the campus that day, I noticed how the students took Devi's admonition to heart. Campus garbage cans were piled high with McDonald's hamburger wrappers and other trash. Hopefully, the lesson stuck and the students maintained good habits of stewardship. After all, *He is coming back and we have to give an account for what He has given us.*

Navy SEAL Admiral William McRaven told a group of graduating students at the University of Texas to *"make their beds every day."* The Admiral, like Devi, was addressing the importance of faithfulness in doing the small tasks we've been given.

McRaven told the students, *"If you can't do the little things right, you'll never be able to do the big things right."*

Faithfulness and Promotion Go Hand-in-Hand

Faithfulness and promotion in the kingdom of God go hand-in-hand. Faithfulness is always rewarded.

In the parable of the talents of silver (Matthew 25), one servant was given five talents of silver. The ESV Study Bible says a talent of silver was worth twenty years of wages for the average worker in Jesus' day. In today's monetary standard, a talent of silver would be worth $10,760. That means that the one-talent man was given a generous amount of money, equal to twenty years' wages, and the five-talent man received a whopping $53,800 from his master.

You see, God has entrusted a whole lot to us, regardless of who we are, and we need to maximize the return on God's investment. That includes our abilities, homes, marriages, families, professions, ministries, and environment. When God entrusted His house to us, He loaned us more than a broken-down hut. He gave us copious amounts of talents, resources, motivations, and abilities. But only by our faithfulness can we grow and multiply His investment.

Proverbs 20:6 says, "Many a man proclaims his own steadfast love, but a faithful man who can find?" That's a good question, isn't it? Who can find a faithful man? I know a lot of talented men who aren't faithful. I also know a lot of men who are handsome, athletic, or smart, but are not consistent. They can't be counted on. But who can find a faithful man?

If you can find a faithful man, you will also find an honest man, someone you can entrust with your property. However, before you bring him on, first check on what his own home and property look like. If he doesn't take care of his own things, you'd better not entrust him with yours.

I know a lot of people who want authority. I have a standing policy: if a man or woman wants authority, don't give it to them before they've demonstrated faithfulness.

When Paul was ready to pass on his teaching to his young disciple, Timothy, he qualified it further by saying, "And what you have heard from me in the presence of many witnesses entrust to faithful men who will be able to teach others also" (2 Timothy 2:2).

Well Done, Good and Faithful Servant

If you've never heard of William Borden, you're not alone. Few have. In a recent article in *Christianity Today*, Borden is

If you can find a faithful man, you will also find an honest man.

referred to as the greatest missionary who never went to a mission field.

William was born in 1887 into a privileged New England family. His father became wealthy in the silver mines of Colorado. When he was seven years old, William, dressed in his best sailor suit, chose to follow the Man from Galilee in what is now called Moody Church in Chicago.

Though earning degrees from both Yale and Princeton, William never wavered in his passion to preach the gospel to the Muslims of China. This scion of wealth taught Bible studies to 1,000 out of the 1,300 students at Yale. He also opened the first rescue mission in New Haven, Connecticut, where he ministered to over 14,000 derelict men. According to the article's author, Jason Casper, Borden's travels took him to over thirty college campuses, trying to rally support for global missions.

His dream of studying Arabic in preparation for a ministry to the Muslims of Gansu Province in China finally came to pass. In early 1913, he sailed to Cairo, Egypt, immediately initiating a campaign to distribute Bibles to all 800,000 inhabitants of Cairo. Three months later, at the age of 25, William succumbed to spinal meningitis. Though he never physically reached the mission field, God counted it as done. Though Abraham never plunged the knife into the beating heart of his son, according to Hebrews 11:19, in God's economy the mission was already accomplished. God considered him faithful. God considered it done.

William Borden's motto was, "No Reserves, No Retreats, No Regrets."

Talk about faithful! Only 25 years of age, but totally faithful to the call of God.

I don't know why stories like this touch me so deeply. I'm crying just repeating his story. I'm touched at the deepest level when I hear of people who give everything to follow Jesus.

I've quit the ministry twice. In 1983, I sat in our apartment in Sarasota, Florida, saying to Devi, "I quit. I can't handle the ministry. I'm just not cut out for it." To emphasize the point, I remember tossing my Bible onto the coffee table. I'm sure God was impressed.

That was on a Tuesday. I vividly recall the day because I got a call on Wednesday from a Hungarian lady who was from a church we formerly pastored in Washington State. In her broken English she said, "Larry, zee Lord He tells me someting. He tells me you quit da ministry. He told me you can't quit zee ministry because He hasn't quit you." Tattle tale. I can't even quit without the Holy Spirit telling on me.

The second time was when I was attending a Promise Keepers stadium event for men in the early nineties in Washington, D.C. Sometime en route to the event, I had decided I'd had enough. I was going to quit the ministry. I was massively discouraged, depressed, and finished with everything. That was it.

At the conclusion of the service, they invited all the pastors to come forward. "Oh, great," I thought, "that's exactly what I don't want to do, come forward to be recognized for something I am no longer going to do." I waited until the very last moment to comply. Nearly all the pastors had gathered at the front. As I made my way to the back of the line, an African-American man said, "Don't drop your sword, Pastor, don't drop your sword." I knew he was an agent of the Holy Spirit. From that moment, I picked up my sword and I haven't dropped it to this day.

Years ago, my good friend, Roy Hicks, Jr., pastor of Faith Center in Eugene, Oregon, told me a story of God speaking to him about his faithfulness. Though Roy has been deceased for many years, I can still hear his voice as if it were yesterday.

He had just finished preaching the last of several morning services, all of which he considered miserable failures. When he approached his car, he began to apologize to the Lord: "I'm so sorry. I did a terrible job today. My preaching was awful." As he described his sense of failure to the Lord, he heard the Lord say, "Roy, I wasn't listening to your sermon, I was watching your faithfulness."

Dear men and women of God, God is more interested in your faithfulness than in your sermons.

God is looking for faithfulness. Faithfulness is the bedrock of character and the very essence of His nature.

When I stand before Jesus on Judgment Day, I know He will not ask me about the size of my congregation, the great things I accomplished, or the amount of money I accumulated or gave away. He is looking for only one thing: "How was your faithfulness?" *If I can hear, "Well done, good and faithful servant," it will be worth it all.*

The Teleios Man: Your Ultimate Identity
Larry Titus

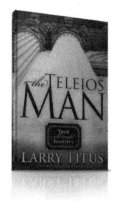

Teleios is Greek for complete, finished, perfection. It's the word Jesus used on the cross when He said, "It is finished." The *teleios* man is the finished, complete man who mirrors the perfection of Christ in every part of his life. He sets an example for generations to follow.

The Teleios Man is written for the man who wakes up in the morning, looks in the mirror, and thinks about who he wants to be for his wife, his kids, his co-workers, himself, and, most importantly, the man he wants to be before God.

The responsibility of it all can be so overwhelming that he may wish that he could just climb back into bed and go back to sleep. That's why he needs to read *The Teleios Man* and receive the empowering encouragement and wisdom that Larry Titus has to share as he mentors men to be the godly, mature, balanced husbands, fathers, and leaders they were born to be!

Order from
www.kingdomglobal.com/store

When Leaders Live Together
Larry Titus—Devi Titus

This is a must-read book for readers with strong A-type personalities or readers who are married to one.

When Leaders Live Together reveals that freedom can be achieved in our relationships as we understand God's purpose for leadership.

As Devi and Larry Titus explore the dynamics of personality and authority, they expose common misconceptions in light of God's Word. Get a copy and learn to live well with your leader!

Order from
www.kingdomglobal.com/store

The Table Experience
Devi Titus

The Table Experience will help you create deeper and more meaningful relationships.

It is full of deep insights and practical applications that will stimulate the reader's intellect and inspire their creativity so that they can enjoy table get-togethers and create emotional bonds that will last a lifetime!

Devi Titus has effectively blended academic and biblical research to show you how to transform your home into a place of peace, a place where love lives, and where relationships thrive and flourish.

Order from
www.kingdomglobal.com/store

The Home Experience
Devi Titus

"Home is where the heart is formed," so slow down. Add beauty and value to everything you do to make your home a place of love and peace.

This full-color, coffee-table style book is both motivating to read and is a mentoring curriculum to use.

The Home Experience is:

- a guide to understanding essential life principles
- an orientation to learn vital relationship skills
- a reference of timeless biblical truths
- a manual of homemaking skills

Learn. Apply. Experience. Restore the dignity and sanctity of your home.

Order from
www.kingdomglobal.com/store